Collins
COBUILD

Active English
Grammar

first edition 2003; reissued 2011

© HarperCollins Publishers 2003, 2011

HarperCollins Publishers
Westerhill Road, Bishopbriggs, Glasgow G64 2QT
Great Britain

www.collinslanguage.com

Collins®, COBUILD® and Bank of English® are registered
trademarks of HarperCollins Publishers Limited

ISBN 978-0-00-742372-9

Editorial Director　　*Managing Editor*
Michela Clari　　　　Maree Airlie

Editors
Gwyneth Fox　Ramesh Krishnamurthy　Jenny Watson
Christina Rammell　Keith Stuart　Alison Macaulay

Publishing Director
Lorna Sinclair Knight

Corpus Acknowledgements

We would like to acknowledge the assistance of the many
hundreds of individuals and companies who have kindly
given permission for copyright material to be used in the
Bank of English. The written sources include many national
and regional newspapers in Britain and overseas; magazine
and periodical publishers; and book publishers in Britain,
the United States, and Australia. Extensive spoken data
has been provided by radio and television broadcasting
companies; research workers at many universities and
other institutions; and numerous individual contributors.
We are grateful to them all.

A catalogue record for this book is available from the
British Library

Computer typeset by Wordcraft, Glasgow

Printed and bound in Italy by Rotolito

INTRODUCTION.

The **Collins COBUILD Active English Grammar** provides learners of English from intermediate level upwards with the grammar they need to know for effective use of English. The most important points of English grammar are explained in a clear, simple way, with hundreds of examples showing grammatical structures in use. The examples have been taken from the Bank of English®, a vast collection of contemporary texts from different sources, totalling over *500 million* words. The Units in **Collins COBUILD Active English Grammar** have been logically organized and there are numerous notes to warn of potential errors. The additional glossary of grammar terms enables learners to fully understand the terminology used, and helps them to master the essential aspects of English grammar.

The attractive colour layout and spacious design makes the **Collins COBUILD Active English Grammar** user-friendly and easily accessible – the ideal reference tool for learners of English.

CONTENTS

LIST OF UNITS

List of Units

List of Units

List of Units

List of Units

List of Units

Registered trademarks
Entered words that we have reason to believe constitute trademarks have been designated as such. However, neither the presence nor absence of such designation should be regarded as affecting the legal status of any trademark.

Clauses and sentences

Main points

Simple sentences have one clause.

Clauses usually consist of a noun group as the subject, and a verb group.

Clauses can also have another noun group as the object or complement.

Clauses can have an adverbial, also called an adjunct.

Changing the order of the words in a clause can change its meaning.

Compound sentences consist of two or more main clauses. Complex sentences always include a subordinate clause, as well as one or more main clauses.

1. A simple sentence has one clause, beginning with a noun group called the subject. The subject is the person or thing that the sentence is about. This is followed by a verb group, which tells you what the subject is doing, or describes the subject's situation.

> *I waited.*
> *The girl screamed.*

Clauses and sentences

2 The verb group may be followed by another noun group, which is called the object. The object is the person or thing affected by the action or situation.

> *He opened <u>the car door.</u>*
> *She married <u>a young engineer.</u>*

After link verbs like 'be', 'become', 'feel', and 'seem', the verb group may be followed by a noun group or an adjective, called a complement. The complement tells you more about the subject.

> *She was <u>a doctor.</u>*
> *He was <u>angry.</u>*

3 The verb group, the object, or the complement can be followed by an adverb or a prepositional phrase, called an adverbial. The adverbial tells you more about the action or situation, for example how, when, or where it happens. Adverbials are also called adjuncts.

> *They shouted <u>loudly.</u>*
> *She won the competition <u>last week.</u>*
> *He was a policeman <u>in Birmingham.</u>*

4 The word order of a clause is different when the clause is a statement, a question, or a command.

> *<u>He speaks</u> English very well.* (statement)
> *<u>Did she win</u> at the Olympics?* (question)
> *<u>Stop</u> her.* (command)

Clauses and sentences

Note that the subject is omitted in commands, so the verb comes first.

5 A compound sentence has two or more main clauses: that is, clauses which are equally important. You join them with 'and', 'but', or 'or'.

> *He met Jane at the station <u>and</u> went shopping.*
> *I wanted to go <u>but</u> I felt too ill.*
> *You can come now <u>or</u> you can meet us there later.*

Note that the order of the two clauses can change the meaning of the sentence.

> *He went shopping <u>and</u> met Jane at the station.*

If the subject of both clauses is the same, you usually omit the subject in the second clause.

> *I wanted to go <u>but felt</u> too ill.*

6 A complex sentence contains a subordinate clause and at least one main clause. A subordinate clause gives information about a main clause, and is introduced by a conjunction such as 'because', 'if', 'that', or a 'wh'-word. Subordinate clauses can come before, after, or inside the main clause.

> <u>*When he stopped,*</u> *no one said anything.*
> <u>*If you want,*</u> *I'll teach you.*

Clauses and sentences

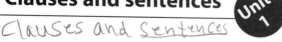

Clauses and Sentences

They were going by car <u>because it was more comfortable.</u>

I told him <u>that nothing was going to happen to me.</u>

The car <u>that I drove</u> was a Ford.

The man <u>who came into the room</u> was small.

The noun group

Main points

Noun groups can be the subject, object, or complement of a verb, or the object of a preposition.

Noun groups can be nouns on their own, but often include other words such as determiners, numbers, and adjectives.

Noun groups can also be pronouns.

Singular noun groups take singular verbs, plural noun groups take plural verbs.

1 Noun groups are used to say which people or things you are talking about. They can be the subject or object of a verb.

> *Strawberries are very expensive now.*
> *Keith likes strawberries.*

A noun group can also be the complement of a link verb such as 'be', 'become', 'feel', or 'seem'.

> *She became champion in 1964*
> *He seemed a nice man.*

A noun group can be used after a preposition, and is often called the object of the preposition.

The noun group

> *I saw him in <u>town.</u>*
> *She was very ill for <u>six months.</u>*

2 A noun group can be a noun on its own, but it often includes other words. A noun group can have a determiner such as 'the' or 'a'. You put determiners at the beginning of the noun group.

> *<u>The girls</u> were not in <u>the house.</u>*
> *He was eating <u>an apple.</u>*

3 A noun group can include an adjective. You usually put the adjective in front of the noun.

> *He was using <u>blue ink.</u>*
> *I like living in <u>a big city.</u>*

Sometimes you can use another noun in front of the noun.

> *I like <u>chocolate cake.</u>*
> *She wanted a job in <u>the oil industry.</u>*

A noun with 's (apostrophe s) is used in front of another noun to show who or what something belongs to or is connected with.

> *I held <u>Sheila's hand</u> very tightly.*
> *He pressed a button on <u>the ship's radio.</u>*

4 A noun group can also have an adverbial, a relative clause, or a 'to'-infinitive clause after it, which makes it more precise.

> *I spoke to <u>a girl in a dark grey dress.</u>*

The noun group

> *She wrote to <u>the man who employed me.</u>*
> *I was trying to think of <u>a way to stop him.</u>*

A common adverbial used after a noun is a prepositional phrase beginning with 'of'.

> *He tied the rope to <u>a large block of stone.</u>*
> *<u>The front door of the house</u> was wide open.*
> *I hated <u>the idea of leaving him alone.</u>*

Participles and some adjectives can also be used after a noun.

➤ See Units 31 and 94.

> *She pointed to <u>the three cards lying on the table.</u>*
> *He is <u>the only man available.</u>*

5 Numbers come after determiners and before adjectives.

> *I had to pay <u>a thousand dollars.</u>*
> *<u>Three tall men</u> came out of the shed.*

6 A noun group can also be a pronoun. You often use a pronoun when you are referring back to a person or thing that you have already mentioned.

> *I've got <u>two boys,</u> and <u>they</u> both enjoy playing football.*

The noun group

You also use a pronoun when you do not know who the person or thing is, or do not want to be precise.

> *Someone is coming to mend it tomorrow.*

7 A noun group can refer to one or more people or things. Many nouns have a singular form referring to one person or thing, and a plural form referring to more than one person or thing. ➤ See Unit 13.

> *My dog never bites people.*
> *She likes dogs.*

Similarly, different pronouns are used in the singular and in the plural.

> *I am going home now.*
> *We want more money.*

When a singular noun group is the subject, it takes a singular verb. When a plural noun group is the subject, it takes a plural verb.

> *His son plays football for the school.*
> *Her letters are always very short.*

The verb group

Main points

In a clause, the verb group usually comes after the subject and always has a main verb.

The main verb has several different forms.

Verb groups can also include one or two auxiliaries, or a modal, or a modal and one or two auxiliaries.

The verb group changes in negative clauses and questions.

Some verb groups are followed by an adverbial, a complement, an object, or two objects.

1. The verb group in a clause is used to say what is happening in an action or situation. You usually put the verb group immediately after the subject. The verb group always includes a main verb.

> I _waited_.
> They _killed_ the elephants.

2. Regular verbs have four forms: the base form, the third person singular form of the present simple, the '-ing' form or present participle, and the '-ed' form used for the past simple and for the past participle.

The verb group

ask	asks	asking	asked
dance	dances	dancing	danced
reach	reaches	reaching	reached
try	tries	trying	tried
dip	dips	dipping	dipped

Irregular verbs may have three forms, four forms, or five forms.

Note that 'be' has eight forms.

cost	costs	costing		
think	thinks	thinking	thought	
swim	swims	swimming	swam	swum
be	am/is/are	being	was/were	been

➤ See pages 442–447 for details of verb forms.

3 The main verb can have one or two auxiliaries in front of it.

> I *had met* him in Zermatt.
> The car *was being repaired*.

The main verb can have a modal in front of it.

> You *can go* now.
> I *would like* to ask you a question.

The main verb can have a modal and one or two auxiliaries in front of it.

> I *could have spent* the whole year on it.
> She *would have been delighted* to see you.

19

The verb group

4 In negative clauses, you have to use a modal or auxiliary and put 'not' after the first word of the verb group.

> He _does not speak_ English very well.
> I _was not smiling._
> It _could not have been_ wrong.

Note that you often use short forms rather than 'not'.

> I _didn't_ know that.
> He _couldn't_ see it.

5 In 'yes/no' questions, you have to put an auxiliary or modal first, then the subject, then the rest of the verb group.

> _Did_ you _meet_ George?
> _Couldn't_ you _have been_ a bit quieter?

In 'wh'-questions, you put the 'wh'-word first. If the 'wh'-word is the subject, you put the verb group next.

> Which _came_ first?
> Who _could have done_ it?

If the 'wh'-word is the object or an adverbial, you must use an auxiliary or modal next, then the subject, then the rest of the verb group.

The verb group

> *What <u>did</u> you <u>do</u>?*
> *Where <u>could</u> she <u>be going</u>?*

6 Some verb groups have an object or two objects after them.

→ See Units 51 and 52.

> *He closed <u>the door.</u>*
> *She sends <u>you her love.</u>*

Verb groups involving link verbs, such as 'be', have a complement after them.

→ See Unit 73.

> *They were <u>sailors.</u>*
> *She felt <u>happy.</u>*

Some verb groups have an adverbial after them.

> *We walked <u>through the park.</u>*
> *She put the letter <u>on the table.</u>*

The imperative and 'let'

Main points

The imperative is the same as the base form of a verb.

You form a negative imperative with 'do not', 'don't', or 'never'.

You use the imperative to ask or tell someone to do something, or to give advice, warnings, or instructions on how to do something.

You use 'let' when you are offering to do something, making suggestions, or telling someone to do something.

1 The imperative is the same as the base form of a verb. You do not use a pronoun in front of it.

> _Come_ to my place.
>
> _Start_ when you hear the bell.

2 You form a negative imperative by putting 'do not', 'don't', or 'never' in front of the verb.

> _Do not write_ in this book.
>
> _Don't go_ so fast.
>
> _Never open_ the front door to strangers.

The imperative and 'let'

3 | You use the imperative when you are:
  ● asking or telling someone to do something

> *<u>Pass</u> the salt.*
> *<u>Hurry up</u>!*

  ● giving someone advice or a warning

> *<u>Mind</u> your head.*
> *<u>Take</u> care!*

  ● giving someone instructions on how to do something

> *<u>Put</u> this bit over here, so it fits into that hole.*
> *<u>Turn</u> right off Broadway into Caxton Street.*

4 | When you want to make an imperative more polite or more emphatic, you can put 'do' in front of it.

> *<u>Do have</u> a chocolate biscuit.*
> *<u>Do stop</u> crying.*
> *<u>Do be</u> careful.*

5 | The imperative is also used in written instructions on how to do something, for example on notices and packets of food, and in books.

> *To report faults, <u>dial</u> 6666.*
> *<u>Store</u> in a dry place.*
> *<u>Fry</u> the chopped onion and pepper in the oil.*

Note that written instructions usually have to be

short. This means that words such as 'the' are often omitted.

Wear rubber gloves.
Turn off switch.
Wipe bulb.

Written imperatives are also used to give warnings.

<u>Reduce</u> speed now.

6 You use 'let me' followed by the base form of a verb when you are offering to do something for someone.

<u>Let me</u> take your coat.
<u>Let me</u> give you a few details.

7 You use 'let's' followed by the base form of a verb when you are suggesting what you and someone else should do.

<u>Let's go</u> outside.
<u>Let's look</u> at our map.

Note that the form 'let us' is only used in formal or written English.

<u>Let us</u> consider a very simple example.

You put 'do' before 'let's' when you are very keen to do something.

The imperative and 'let'

> *Do let's get a taxi.*

The negative of 'let's' is 'let's not' or 'don't let's'.

> *Let's not talk about that.*
> *Don't let's actually write it in the book.*

8 You use 'let' followed by a noun group and the base form of a verb when you are telling someone to do something or to allow someone else to do it.

> *Let me see it.*
> *Let Philip have a look at it.*

Questions

Main points

In most questions the first verb comes before the subject.

'Yes/no'-questions begin with an auxiliary or a modal.

'Wh'-questions begin with a 'wh'-word.

1 Questions which can be answered 'yes' or 'no' are called 'yes/no'-questions.

> *'Are you ready?' – 'Yes.'*
> *'Have you read this magazine?' – 'No.'*

If the verb group has more than one word, the first word comes at the beginning of the sentence, before the subject. The rest of the verb group comes after the subject.

> *<u>Is he</u> coming?*
> *<u>Can John</u> swim?*
> *<u>Will you</u> have finished by lunchtime?*
> *<u>Couldn't you</u> have been a bit quieter?*
> *<u>Has he</u> been working?*

2 If the verb group consists of only a main verb, you use the auxiliary 'do', 'does', or 'did' at the beginning

Questions

of the sentence, before the subject. After the subject you use the base form of the verb.

> *<u>Do the British</u> take sport seriously?*
> *<u>Does that</u> sound like anyone you know?*
> *<u>Did he</u> go to the fair?*

Note that when the main verb is 'do', you still have to add 'do', 'does', or 'did' before the subject.

> *<u>Do they</u> do the work themselves?*
> *<u>Did you</u> do an 'O' Level in German?*

3 If the main verb is 'have', you usually put 'do', 'does', or 'did' before the subject.

> *<u>Does anyone have</u> a question?*
> *<u>Did you have</u> a good flight?*

When 'have' means 'own' or 'possess', you can put it before the subject, without using 'do', 'does', or 'did', but this is less common.

> *<u>Has he</u> any idea what it's like?*

4 If the main verb is the present simple or past simple of 'be', you put the verb at the beginning of the sentence, before the subject.

> *<u>Are you</u> ready?*
> *<u>Was it</u> lonely without us?*

5 When you want someone to give you more information than just 'yes' or 'no', you ask a 'wh'-question, which begins with a 'wh'-word:

what	when	where	which
who	whom	whose	why
how			

Note that 'whom' is only used in formal English.

6 When a 'wh'-word is the subject of a question, the 'wh'-word comes first, then the verb group. You do not add 'do', 'does', or 'did' as an auxiliary.

> _What_ happened?
> _Which_ is the best restaurant?
> _Who_ could have done it?

7 When a 'wh'-word is the object of a verb or preposition, the 'wh'-word comes first, then you follow the rules for 'yes/no'-questions, adding 'do', 'does', or 'did' where necessary.

> _How many_ are there?
> _Which_ do you like best?

If there is a preposition, it comes at the end. However, you always put the preposition before 'whom'.

> _What_'s this _for?_
> _With whom_ were you talking?

Questions

Note that you follow the same rules as for 'wh'-words as objects when the question begins with 'when', 'where', 'why', or 'how'.

> *When* would you be coming down?
> *Why* did you do it?
> *Where* did you get that *from?*

8 You can also use 'what', 'which', 'whose', 'how many', and 'how much' with a noun.

> *Whose idea* was it?
> *How much money* have we got in the bank?

You can use 'which', 'how many', and 'how much' with 'of' and a noun group.

> *Which of* the suggested answers was the correct one?
> *How many of* them bothered to come?

➤ See Unit 6 for more information on 'wh'-words.

Main points

You use 'who', 'whom', and 'whose' to ask about people, and 'which' to ask about people or things.

You use 'what' to ask about things, and 'what for' to ask about reasons and purposes.

You use 'how' to ask about the way something happens.

You use 'when' to ask about times, 'why' to ask about reasons, and 'where' to ask about places and directions.

1 You use 'who', 'whom', or 'whose' in questions about people. 'Who' is used to ask questions about the subject or object of the verb, or about the object of a preposition.

> *Who discovered this?*
> *Who did he marry?*
> *Who did you dance with?*

In formal English, 'whom' is used as the object of a verb or preposition. The preposition always comes in front of 'whom'.

'Wh'-questions

Whom did you see?
For whom were they supposed to do it?

You use 'whose' to ask which person something belongs to or is related to. 'Whose' can be the subject or the object.

Whose is nearer?
Whose did you prefer, hers or mine?

2. You use 'which' to ask about one person or thing, out of a number of people or things. 'Which' can be the subject or object.

Which is your son?
Which does she want?

3. You use 'what' to ask about things, for example about actions and events. 'What' can be the subject or object.

What has happened to him?
What is he selling?
What will you talk about?

You use 'what…for' to ask about the reason for an action, or the purpose of an object.

What are you going there for?
What are those lights for?

4. You use 'how' to ask about the way in which something happens or is done.

How did you know we were coming?
How are you going to get home?

You also use 'how' to ask about the way a person or thing feels or looks.

'How are you?' – *'Well, how do I look?'*

5 'How' is also used:

● with adjectives to ask about the degree of quality that someone or something has

How good are you at Maths?
How hot shall I make the curry?

● with adjectives such as 'big', 'old', and 'far' to ask about size, age, and distance

How old are your children?
How far is it to Montreal from here?

Note that you do not normally use 'How small', 'How young', or 'How near'.

● with adverbs such as 'long' and 'often' to ask about time, or 'well' to ask about abilities

How long have you lived here?
How well can you read?

● with 'many' and 'much' to ask about the number or amount of something

'Wh'-questions

How many were there?
How much did he tell you?

6 You use 'when' to ask about points in time or periods of time, 'why' to ask about the reason for an action, and 'where' to ask about place and direction.

When are you coming home?
When were you in London?
Why are you here?
Where is the station?
Where are you going?

You can also ask about direction using 'which direction…in' or 'which way'.

Which direction did he go _in?_
Which way did he go?

Question tags: forms

Main points

You add a question tag to a statement to turn it into a question.

A question tag consists of a verb and a pronoun. The verb in a question tag is always an auxiliary, a modal, or a form of the main verb 'be'.

With a positive statement, you usually use a negative question tag containing a short form ending in '-n't'.

With a negative statement, you always use a positive question tag.

1 A question tag is a short phrase that is added to the end of a statement to turn it into a 'yes/no'-question. You use question tags when you want to ask someone to confirm or disagree with what you are saying, or when you want to sound more polite. Question tags are rarely used in formal written English.

> *He's very friendly, <u>isn't he?</u>*
> *You haven't seen it before, <u>have you?</u>*

Question tags: forms

2 You form a question tag by using an auxiliary, a modal, or a form of the main verb 'be', followed by a pronoun. The pronoun refers to the subject of the statement.

> *David's school is quite nice, <u>isn't it?</u>*
> *She made a really remarkable recovery, <u>didn't she?</u>*
> *I should give her a ring, <u>shouldn't I?</u>*

3 If the statement contains an auxiliary or modal, the same auxiliary or modal is used in the question tag.

> *Jill<u>'s</u> coming tomorrow, <u>isn't</u> she?*
> *You <u>did</u>n't know I was an artist, <u>did</u> you?*
> *You<u>'ve</u> never been to Benidorm, <u>have</u> you?*
> *You <u>will</u> stay in touch, <u>won't</u> you?*

4 If the statement does not contain an auxiliary, a modal, or 'be' as a main verb, you use 'do', 'does', or 'did' in the question tag.

> *You <u>like</u> it here, <u>do</u>n't you?*
> *Sally still <u>works</u> there, <u>doesn't</u> she?*
> *He <u>played</u> for Ireland, <u>did</u>n't he?*

5 If the statement contains the present simple or

Question tags: forms

past simple of 'be' as a main verb, the same form of the verb 'be' is used in the question tag.

> It _is_ quite warm, _isn't_ it?
> They _were_ really rude, _weren't_ they?

6 If the statement contains the simple present or simple past of 'have' as a main verb, you usually use 'do', 'does', or 'did' in the question tag.

> He _has_ a problem, _doesn't_ he?
> She _had_ a bath yesterday, _didn't_ she?

You can also use the same form of 'have' in the question tag.

> She _has_ a large house, _hasn't_ she?
> You _haven't_ any stamps, _have_ you?

7 With a positive statement you normally use a negative question tag, formed by adding '-n't' to the verb.

> You _like_ Ralph a lot, _don't_ you?
> They _are_ beautiful, _aren't_ they?

Note that the negative question tag with 'I' and the verb 'to be' is 'aren't'.

> _I'm_ a fool, _aren't I?_

Question tags: forms

8 With a negative statement you always use a positive question tag.

> It <u>doesn't</u> work, <u>does</u> it?
> You <u>won't</u> tell anyone else, <u>will</u> you?
> You <u>haven't</u> been there before, <u>have</u> you?

Main points

You can use negative statements with positive question tags to make requests.

You use positive statements with positive question tags to show reactions.

You use some question tags to make imperatives more polite.

1 You can use a negative statement and a positive question tag to ask people for things, or to ask for help or information.

> *You <u>wouldn't</u> sell it to me, <u>would</u> you?*
> *You <u>won't</u> tell anyone else this, <u>will</u> you?*

2 When you want to show your reaction to what someone has just said, for example by expressing interest, surprise, doubt, or anger, you use a positive statement with a positive question tag.

> *You'<u>ve</u> been to North America before, <u>have you?</u>*
> *You <u>fell</u> on your back, <u>did you?</u>*
> *I borrowed your car last night. – Oh, you <u>did, did you?</u>*

Question tags: uses

3 When you use an imperative, you can be more polite by adding one of the following question tags.

> will you   won't you   would you

> *See* that she gets safely back, *won't you?*
> *Look* at that, *would you?*

When you use a negative imperative, you can only use 'will you' as a question tag.

> *Don't* tell Howard, *will you?*

'Will you' and 'won't you' can also be used to emphasize anger or impatience. 'Can't you' is also used in this way.

> *Oh, hurry up, will you!*
> *For goodness sake be quiet, can't you!*

4 You use the question tag 'shall we' when you make a suggestion using 'let's'.

> *Let's* forget it, *shall we?*

You use the question tag 'shall I' after 'I'll'.

> *I'll* tell you, *shall I?*

5 You use 'they' in question tags after 'anybody', 'anyone', 'everybody', 'everyone', 'nobody', 'no one', 'somebody' or 'someone'.

Everyone will be leaving on Friday, won't *they?*
Nobody had bothered to plant new ones, had *they?*

You use 'it' in question tags after 'anything', 'everything', 'nothing', or 'something'.

Nothing matters now, does *it?*
Something should be done, shouldn't *it?*

You use 'there' in question tags after 'there is', 'there are', 'there was', or 'there were'.

There's a new course out now, isn't *there?*

6 When you are replying to a question tag, your answer refers to the statement, not the question tag.

If you want to confirm a positive statement, you say 'yes'. For example, if you have finished a piece of work and someone says to you 'You've finished that, haven't you?', the answer is 'yes'.

'It became stronger, didn't it?' – 'Yes, it did.'

If you want to disagree with a positive statement, you say 'no'. For example, if you have not finished your work and someone says 'You've finished that, haven't you?', the answer is 'no'.

You've just seen a performance of the play, haven't you? – No, not yet.

Question tags: uses

If you want to confirm a negative statement, you say 'no'. For example, if you have not finished your work and someone says 'You haven't finished that, have you?', the answer is 'no'.

> 'You <u>didn't know</u> that, did you?' – '<u>No.</u>'

If you want to disagree with a negative statement, you say 'yes'. For example, if you have finished a piece of work and someone says 'You haven't finished that, have you?', the answer is 'yes'.

> 'You <u>haven't been</u> there, have you?' – '<u>Yes</u>, I have.'

Indirect questions

Main points

You use indirect questions to ask for information or help.

In indirect questions, the subject of the question comes before the verb.

You can use 'if' or 'whether' in indirect questions.

1 When you ask someone for information, you can use an indirect question beginning with a phrase such as 'Could you tell me…' or 'Do you know…'.

> _Could you tell me_ how far it is to the nearest bank?
> _Do you know_ where Jane is?

2 When you want to ask someone politely to do something, you can use an indirect question after 'I wonder'.

> _I wonder_ if you can help me.

Indirect questions

> *I was wondering whether you could give me some information?*

You also use 'I wonder' followed by an indirect question to indicate what you are thinking about.

> *I wonder what she'll look like.*
> *I wonder which hotel it was.*
> *I just wonder what you make of all that.*

3 In indirect questions, the subject of the question comes before the verb, just as it does in affirmative sentences.

> *Do you know where Jane is?*
> *I wonder if you can help me.*
> *She asked me why I was late.*

4 You do not normally use the auxiliary 'do' in indirect questions.

> *Can you remember when they open on Sundays?*
> *I wonder what he feels about it.*

The auxiliary 'do' can be used in indirect questions, but only for emphasis, or to make a contrast with

43

something that has already been said. It is not put before the subject as in direct questions.

> *I was beginning to wonder if he <u>does</u> do anything.*
> *He wondered whether it really <u>did</u> make any difference to the outcome.*

5 You use 'if' or 'whether' to introduce indirect questions.

> *I wonder <u>if</u> you'd give the children a bath tonight?*
> *I'm writing to ask <u>whether</u> you would care to come and visit us.*

'Whether' is used especially when there is a choice of possibilities.

> *I wonder <u>whether</u> it is the police or just a neighbour.*
> *I wonder <u>whether</u> that is good for him or not.*

Note that you can put 'or not' immediately after 'whether', but not immediately after 'if'.

Indirect questions

I wonder <u>whether or not</u> we are so different from our ancestors.
Even optimists wonder <u>if</u> property prices can keep on rising.

Main points

A short answer uses an auxiliary, a modal, or the main verb 'be'.

A short answer can be in the form of a statement or a question.

1 Short answers are very common in spoken English. For example, when someone asks you a 'yes/no'-question, you can give a short answer by using a pronoun with an auxiliary, modal, or the main verb 'be'. You usually put 'yes' or 'no' before the short answer.

> '_Does_ she still want to come?' – 'Yes, _she does._'
> '_Can_ you imagine what it might feel like?' – 'No, _I can't._'
> '_Are_ you married?' – '_I am._'

Note that a short answer such as 'Yes, I will' is more polite or friendly than just 'Yes', or than repeating all the words used in the question. People often repeat all the words used in the question when they feel angry or impatient.

Short answers

'Will you have finished by lunchtime?' – *'Yes, I will have finished by lunchtime.'*

2 You can also use short answers to agree or disagree with what someone says.

'You don't like Joan?' – *'No, I don't.'*
'I'm not coming with you.' – *'Yes, you are.'*

If the statement that you are commenting on does not contain an auxiliary, modal, or the main verb 'be', you use a form of 'do' in the short answer.

'He never comes on time.' – *'Oh yes he does.'*

3 You often reply to what has been said by using a short question.

'He's not in Japan now.' – *'Oh, isn't he?'*
'He gets free meals.' – *'Does he?'*

Note that questions like these are not always asked to get information, but are often used to express your reaction to what has been said, for example to show interest or surprise.

'Dad doesn't help me at all.' – *'Doesn't he? Why not?'*
'Penny has been climbing before.' – *'Oh, has she? When was that?'*

4 If you want to show that you definitely agree with a positive statement that someone has just made, you can use a negative short question.

> *'Well, that was very nice.'* – *'Yes, <u>wasn't it?</u>'*

5 When you want to ask for more information, you can use a 'wh'-word on its own or with a noun as a short answer.

> *'He saw a snake.'* – *'<u>Where?</u>'*
> *'He knew my cousin.'* – *'<u>Which cousin?</u>'*

You can also use 'Which one' and 'Which ones'.

> *'Can you pass me the cup?'* – *'<u>Which one?</u>'*

6 Sometimes a statement about one person also applies to another person. When this is the case, you can use a short answer with 'so' for positive statements, and with 'neither' or 'nor' for negative statements, using the same verb that was used in the statement.

You use 'so', 'neither', or 'nor' with an auxiliary, modal, or the main verb 'be'. The verb comes before the subject.

> *'You were different then.'* – *'<u>So were you.</u>'*
> *'I don't normally drink at lunch.'* – *'<u>Neither do I.</u>'*
> *'I can't do it.'* – *'<u>Nor can I.</u>'*

Short answers

You can use 'not either' instead of 'neither', in which case the verb comes after the subject.

> *'He doesn't understand.' – 'We don't either.'*

7 You often use 'so' in short answers after verbs such as 'think', 'hope', 'expect', 'imagine', and 'suppose', when you think that the answer to the question is 'yes'.

> *'You'll be home at six?' – 'I hope so.'*
> *'So it was worth doing?' – 'I suppose so.'*

You use 'I'm afraid so' when you are sorry that the answer is 'yes'.

> *'Is it raining?' – 'I'm afraid so.'*

With 'suppose', 'think', 'imagine', or 'expect' in short answers, you also form negatives with 'so'.

> *'Will I see you again?' – 'I don't suppose so.'*
> *'Is Barry Knight a golfer?' – 'No, I don't think so.'*

However, you say 'I hope not' and 'I'm afraid not'.

> *'It isn't empty, is it?' – 'I hope not.'*

Sentences with 'not'

Main points

'Not' is often shortened to '-n't' and added to some verbs.

You put 'not' after the first verb in the verb group, or you use a short form.

1 In spoken and in informal written English, 'not' is often shortened to '-n't' and added to an auxiliary, a modal, or a form of the main verb 'be'.

> I _haven't_ heard from her recently.
> I _wasn't_ angry.

Here is a list of short forms.

isn't	haven't	don't	can't	shan't	daren't
aren't	hasn't	doesn't	couldn't	shouldn't	needn't
wasn't	hadn't	didn't	mightn't	won't	
weren't			mustn't	wouldn't	
			oughtn't		

If the verb is already shortened, you cannot add '-n't'.

> It_'s not_ easy.
> I_'ve not_ had time.

50

Sentences with 'not'

You cannot add '-n't' to 'am'. You use 'I'm not'.

> *I'm not* excited.

2 If the verb group has more than one word, you put 'not' after the first word, or you use a short form.

> I *was not* smiling.
> He *hadn't* attended many meetings.
> They *might not* notice.
> I *haven't* been playing football recently.

3 If the sentence only contains a main verb other than 'be', you use the auxiliary 'do'.

You use 'do not', 'does not', 'did not', or a short form, followed by the base form of the main verb.

> They *do not need* to talk.
> He *does not speak* English very well.
> I *didn't know* that.

Note that if the main verb is 'do', you still use a form of 'do' as an auxiliary.

> They *didn't do* anything about it.

4 If the main verb is the present or past simple of 'be', you put 'not' immediately after it, or you use a short form.

> It *is not* difficult to understand.

Sentences with 'not'

> *It's <u>not</u> the same, is it?*
> *He <u>wasn't</u> a bad actor actually.*

5 If the main verb is 'have', you usually use a form of 'do' as an auxiliary.

> *They <u>don't have</u> any money.*

You can also use a short form, or you can put 'not' after the verb but this is not very common.

> *He <u>hadn't</u> enough money.*

6 You can put 'not' in front of an '-ing' form or a 'to'-infinitive.

> *We stood there, <u>not knowing</u> what to do.*
> *Try <u>not to worry</u>.*

7 In negative questions, you use a short form.

> *Why <u>didn't</u> she win at the Olympics?*
> *<u>Hasn't</u> he put on weight?*
> *<u>Aren't</u> you bored?*

8 You can use a negative question:

● to express your feelings, for example to show that you are surprised or disappointed

> *Hasn't he done it yet?*

Sentences with 'not'

● in exclamations

Isn't the weather awful!

● when you think you know something and you just want someone to agree with you

'Aren't you Joanne's brother?' – 'Yes, I am.'

9 Note the meaning of 'yes' and 'no' in answers to negative questions.

> *'Isn't Tracey going to get a bit bored in Birmingham?'*
> – *'Yes.'* (She is going to get bored.)
> – *'No.'* (She is not going to get bored.)

Negative words

Main points

A negative sentence contains a negative word.

You do not normally use two negative words in the same clause.

---

1. Negative statements contain a negative word.

not	nobody	neither
never	no one	nor
no	nothing	
none	nowhere	

➤ See Unit 11 for negative statements using 'not'.

2. You use 'never' to say that something was not the case at any time, or will not be the case at any time.

If the verb group has more than one word, you put 'never' after the first word.

I've never had such a horrible meal.
He could never trust her again.

3. If the only verb in the sentence is the present simple or past simple of any main verb except 'be', you put 'never' before the verb.

Negative words

She <u>never goes</u> abroad.
He <u>never went</u> to university.

If the only verb in the sentence is the simple present or simple past of the main verb 'be', you normally put 'never' after the verb.

He<u>'s never</u> late.
There <u>were never</u> any people in the house.

You can also use 'never' at the beginning of an imperative sentence.

<u>Never</u> walk alone late at night.

4 You use 'no' before a noun to say that something does not exist or is not available.

He has given <u>no</u> reason for his decision.
The island has <u>no</u> trees at all.

Note that if there is another negative word in the clause, you use 'any', not 'no'.

It won<u>'t</u> do <u>any</u> good.

5 You use 'none' or 'none of' to say that there is not even one thing or person, or not even a small amount of something.

You can't go to a college here because there are <u>none</u> in this area.

'Where's the coffee?' – 'There's <u>none</u> left.'
<u>None of</u> us understood the play.

➤ See Unit 27 for more information on 'none' and 'none of'.

6 | You also use 'nobody', 'no one', 'nothing', and 'nowhere' in negative statements.

You use 'nobody' or 'no one' to talk about people.

<u>Nobody</u> in her house knows any English.
<u>No one</u> knew.

'No one' can also be written 'no-one'.

There's <u>no-one</u> here.

You use 'nothing' to talk about things.

There's <u>nothing</u> you can do.

You use 'nowhere' to talk about places.

There's almost <u>nowhere</u> left to go.

➤ See Unit 21 for more information about these words.

7 | You do not normally use two negative words in the same clause. For example, you do not say 'Nobody could see nothing'. You say 'Nobody could see anything'.

You use 'anything', 'anyone', 'anybody', and 'anywhere' instead of 'nothing', 'no one', 'nobody', and

Negative words

'nowhere' when the clause already contains a negative word.

> *No-one* can find Howard or Barbara *anywhere.*
> I could *never* discuss *anything* with them.

8 The only negative words that are often used together in the same clause are 'neither' and 'nor'.

You use 'neither' and 'nor' together to say that two alternatives are not possible, not likely, or not true.

> *Neither* Margaret *nor* John was there.
> They had *neither* food *nor* money.

Count nouns

Main points

Count nouns have two forms, singular and plural.

They can be used with numbers.

Singular count nouns always take a determiner.

Plural count nouns do not need a determiner.

Singular count nouns take a singular verb and plural count nouns take a plural verb.

In English, some things are thought of as individual items that can be counted directly. The nouns which refer to these countable things are called count nouns. Most nouns in English are count nouns.

▶ See Unit 15 for information on uncount nouns.

1 Count nouns have two forms. The singular form refers to one thing or person.

>   …*a book* … …*the teacher*.

The plural form refers to more than one thing or person.

>   … <u>*books*</u> … …*some <u>teachers.</u>*

Count nouns

2 You add '-s' to form the plural of most nouns.

book → books	school → schools		

You add '-es' to nouns ending in '-ss', '-ch', '-s', '-sh', or '-x'.

class → classes	watch → watches
gas → gases	dish → dishes
fox → foxes	

Some nouns ending in '-o' add '-s', and some add '-es'.

photo → photos	piano → pianos
hero → heroes	potato → potatoes

Nouns ending in a consonant and '-y' change to '-ies'.

country → countries	lady → ladies
party → parties	victory → victories

Nouns ending in a vowel and '-y' add an '-s'.

boy → boys	day → days
key → keys	valley → valleys

Count nouns

Some common nouns have irregular plurals.

child	→	children	foot	→	feet
man	→	men	mouse	→	mice
tooth	→	teeth	woman	→	women

⊖ WARNING: Some nouns that end in '-s' are uncount nouns, for example 'athletics' and 'physics'. ➤ See Unit 15.

3 Count nouns can be used with numbers.

> *… one table…*   *… two cats…*
> *… three hundred pounds.*

4 Singular count nouns cannot be used alone, but always take a determiner such as 'a', 'another', 'every', or 'the'.

> *We've killed <u>a</u> pig.*
> *He was eating <u>another</u> apple.*
> *I parked <u>the</u> car over there.*

5 Plural count nouns can be used with or without a determiner. They do not take a determiner when they refer to things or people in general.

> *Does the hotel have <u>large rooms</u>?*
> *The film is not suitable for <u>children.</u>*

Plural count nouns do take a determiner when they refer precisely to particular things or people.

Count nouns

> *Our computers are very expensive.*
> *These cakes are delicious.*

➤ See Unit 23 for more information on determiners.

6 When a count noun is the subject of a verb, a singular count noun takes a singular verb.

> *My son likes playing football.*
> *The address on the letter was wrong.*

A plural count noun takes a plural verb.

> *Bigger cars cost more.*
> *I thought more people were coming.*

➤ See also Unit 14 on collective nouns.

Main points

Singular nouns are used only in the singular, always with a determiner.

Plural nouns are used only in the plural, some with a determiner.

Collective nouns can be used with singular or plural verbs.

1. Some nouns are used in particular meanings in the singular with a determiner, like count nouns, but are not used in the plural with that meaning. They are often called 'singular nouns'.

   Some of these nouns are normally used with 'the' because they refer to things that are unique.

air	country	countryside	dark
daytime	end	future	ground
moon	past	sea	seaside
sky	sun	wind	world

   The sun was shining.
   I am scared of *the dark.*

   Other singular nouns are normally used with 'a' because they refer to things that we usually talk

Singular and plural

about one at a time.

bath	chance	drink	fight	go
jog	move	rest	ride	
run	shower	smoke	snooze	
start	walk	wash		

I went upstairs and had <u>a wash.</u>
Why don't we go outside for <u>a smoke?</u>

2. Some nouns are used in particular meanings in the plural with or without determiners, like count nouns, but are not used in the singular with that meaning. They are often called 'plural nouns'.

His <u>clothes</u> looked terribly dirty.
<u>Troops</u> are being sent in today.

Some of these nouns are always used with determiners.

activities	authorities	feelings	likes
pictures	sights	travels	

I went to <u>the pictures</u> with Tina.
You hurt <u>his feelings.</u>

Some are usually used without determiners.

airs	expenses	goods	refreshments	riches

<u>Refreshments</u> are available inside.
They have agreed to pay for travel and <u>expenses.</u>

Singular and plural

⊖ WARNING: 'Police' is a plural noun, but does not end in '-s'.

The <u>police</u> were informed immediately.

3 A small group of plural nouns refer to single items that have two linked parts. They refer to tools that people use or things that people wear.

binoculars	pincers	pliers	scales
scissors	shears	tweezers	glasses
jeans	knickers	pants	pyjamas
shorts	tights	trousers	

She was wearing brown <u>trousers.</u>
These <u>scissors</u> are sharp.

You can use 'a pair of' to make it clear you are talking about one item, or a number with 'pairs of' when you are talking about several items.

I was sent out to buy <u>a pair of scissors.</u>
Liza had given me <u>three pairs of jeans.</u>

Note that you also use 'a pair of' with words such as 'gloves', 'shoes', and 'socks' that you often talk about in twos.

4 With some nouns that refer to a group of people or things, the same form can be used with singular or plural verbs, because you can think of the group as a unit or as individuals. Similarly, you can use sin-

Singular and plural

gular or plural pronouns to refer back to them. These nouns are often called 'collective nouns'.

army	audience	committee	company
crew	data	enemy	family
flock	gang	government	group
herd	media	navy	press
public	staff	team	

Our little <u>group is</u> complete again.
Our <u>family isn't</u> poor any more.
The largest <u>group are</u> the boys.
My <u>family are</u> perfectly normal.

The names of many organizations and sports teams are also collective nouns, but are normally used with plural verbs in spoken English.

<u>The BBC is</u> showing the programme on Saturday.
<u>The BBC are</u> planning to use the new satellite.
<u>Liverpool is</u> leading 1-0.
<u>Liverpool are</u> attacking again.

Uncount nouns

Main points

Uncount nouns have only one form, and take a singular verb.

They are not used with 'a', or with numbers.

Some nouns can be both uncount nouns and count nouns.

1 English speakers think that some things cannot be counted directly. The nouns which refer to these uncountable things are called uncount nouns. Uncount nouns often refer to:

substances:	coal food ice iron rice steel water
human qualities:	courage cruelty honesty patience
feelings:	anger happiness joy pride relief respect
activities:	aid help sleep travel work
abstract ideas:	beauty death freedom fun life luck

Uncount nouns

> *The donkey needed <u>food</u> and <u>water.</u>*
> *Soon, they lost <u>patience</u> and sent me to Durban.*
> *I was greeted with shouts of <u>joy.</u>*
> *All prices include <u>travel</u> to and from London.*
> *We talked for hours about <u>freedom.</u>*

▶ See Unit 13 for information on count nouns.

2. Uncount nouns have only one form. They do not have a plural form.

> *I needed <u>help</u> with my homework.*
> *The children had great <u>fun</u> playing with the puppets.*

⊖ WARNING: Some nouns which are uncount nouns in English have plurals in other languages.

advice	baggage	equipment	furniture
homework	information	knowledge	luggage
machinery	money	news	traffic

> *We want to spend more <u>money</u> on roads.*
> *Soldiers carried so much <u>equipment</u> that they were barely able to move.*

Uncount nouns

3 Some uncount nouns end in '-s' and therefore look like plural count nouns. They usually refer to:

subjects of study:	maths	physics
activities:	athletics	gymnastics
games:	cards	darts
illnesses:	measles	mumps

> _Mathematics_ is too difficult for me.
> _Measles_ is in most cases a harmless illness.

4 When an uncount noun is the subject of a verb, it takes a singular verb.

> _Electricity <u>is</u> dangerous._
> _Food <u>was</u> very expensive in those days._

5 Uncount nouns are not used with 'a'.

> _They resent having to pay <u>money</u> to people like me._
> _My father started <u>work</u> when he was ten._

Uncount nouns are used with 'the' when they refer to something that is specified or known.

> _I am interested in <u>the education of young children.</u>_
> _She buried <u>the money that Hilary had given her.</u>_

6 Uncount nouns are not used with numbers. However, you can often refer to a quantity of something

Uncount nouns

which is expressed by an uncount noun, by using a word like 'some'.

➤ See Unit 23.

> *Please buy <u>some bread</u> when you go to town.*
> *Let me give you <u>some advice.</u>*

Some uncount nouns that refer to food or drink can be count nouns when they refer to quantities of the food or drink.

> *Do you like <u>coffee?</u>* (uncount)
> *We asked for <u>two coffees.</u>* (count)

Uncount nouns are often used with expressions such as 'a loaf of', 'packets of', or 'a piece of', to talk about a quantity or an item. 'A bit of' is common in spoken English.

> *I bought <u>two loaves of bread</u> yesterday.*
> *He gave me <u>a</u> very good <u>piece of advice.</u>*
> *They own <u>a bit of land</u> near Cambridge.*

7 Some nouns are uncount nouns when they refer to something in general and count nouns when they refer to a particular instance of something.

> *<u>Victory</u> was now assured.* (uncount)
> *In 1960, the party won <u>a convincing victory</u>.*
> (count)

Personal pronouns

Main points

You use personal pronouns to refer back to something or someone that has already been mentioned.

You also use personal pronouns to refer to people and things directly.

There are two sets of personal pronouns: subject pronouns and object pronouns.

You can use 'you' and 'they' to refer to people in general.

1 When something or someone has already been mentioned, you refer to them again by using a pronoun.

> John took <u>the book</u> and opened <u>it.</u>
> He rang <u>Mary</u> and invited <u>her</u> to dinner.
> 'Have you been to <u>London</u>?' – 'Yes, <u>it</u> was very crowded.'
> <u>My father</u> is fat – <u>he</u> weighs over fifteen stone.

In English, 'he' and 'she' normally refer to people, occasionally to animals, but very rarely to things.

Personal pronouns

2 You use a pronoun to refer directly to people or things that are present or are involved in the situation you are in.

> *Where shall we meet, Sally?*
> *I do the washing; he does the cooking; we share the washing-up.*
> *Send us a card so we'll know where you are.*

3 There are two sets of personal pronouns, subject pronouns and object pronouns. You use subject pronouns as the subject of a verb.

I	you	he	she	it	we	they

Note that 'you' is used for the singular and plural form.

> *We are going there later.*
> *I don't know what to do.*

4 You use object pronouns as the direct or indirect object of a verb.

me	you	him	her	it	us	them

Note that 'you' is used for the singular and plural form.

> *The nurse washed me with cold water.*
> *The ball hit her in the face.*

Personal pronouns

> *John showed <u>him</u> the book.*
> *Can you give <u>me</u> some more cake?*

Note that, in modern English, you use object pronouns rather than subject pronouns after the verb 'be'.

> *'Who is it?' – 'It<u>'s me.</u>'*
> *There <u>was</u> only John, Baz, and <u>me</u> in the room.*

You also use object pronouns as the object of a preposition.

> *We were all sitting in a cafe <u>with him.</u>*
> *Did you give it <u>to them?</u>*

5 You can use 'you' and 'they' to talk about people in general.

> <u>*You*</u> *have to drive on the other side of the road on the continent.*
> <u>*They*</u> *say she's very clever.*

6 You can use 'it' as an impersonal subject in general statements which refer to the time, the date, or the weather.
➤ See Unit 17.

> *'What time is <u>it?</u>' '<u>It</u>'s half past three.'*
> <u>*It*</u> *is January 19th.*
> <u>*It*</u> *is rainy and cold.*

Personal pronouns

You can also use 'it' as the subject or object in general statements about a situation.

> *<u>It</u> is too far to walk.*
> *I like <u>it</u> here. Can we stay a bit longer?*

7 A singular pronoun usually refers back to a singular noun group, and a plural pronoun to a plural noun group. However, you can use plural pronouns to refer back to:

● indefinite pronouns, even though they are always followed by a singular verb

> *If <u>anybody comes,</u> tell <u>them</u> I'm not in.*

● collective nouns, even when you have used a singular verb

> *His <u>family was</u> waiting in the next room, but <u>they</u> had not yet been informed.*

Impersonal subject 'it'

Main points

You use impersonal 'it' as the subject of a sentence to introduce new information.

You use 'it' to talk about the time or the date.

You use 'it' to talk about the weather.

You use 'it' to express opinions about places, situations, and events.

'It' is often used with the passive of reporting verbs to express general beliefs and opinions.

---

1 'It' is a pronoun. As a personal pronoun it refers back to something that has already been mentioned.

> *They learn to speak <u>English</u> before they learn to read <u>it.</u>*
> *<u>Maybe he changed his mind,</u> but I doubt <u>it.</u>*

You can also use 'it' as the subject of a sentence when it does not refer back to anything that has already been mentioned. This impersonal use of 'it' introduces new information, and is used particularly to talk about times, dates, the weather, and personal opinions.

Impersonal subject 'it'

2 You use impersonal 'it' with a form of 'be' to talk about the time or the date.

> _It is_ nearly one o'clock.
> _It's_ the sixth of April today.

3 You use impersonal 'it' with verbs which refer to the weather:

| drizzle | hail | pour | rain | sleet | snow | thunder |

> _It's_ still _raining._
> _It snowed_ steadily through the night.
> _It was pouring_ with rain.

You can describe the weather by using 'it' followed by 'be' and an adjective with or without a noun.

> _It's a lovely day._
> _It was very bright._

You can describe a change in the weather by using 'it' followed by 'get' and an adjective.

> _It was getting cold._
> _It's getting dark._

4 You use impersonal 'it', followed by a form of 'be' and an adjective or noun group, to express your opinion about a place, a situation, or an event. The adjective or noun group can be followed by an adverbial or by an '-ing' clause, a 'to'-infinitive clause, or a 'that'-clause.

> *It was* terribly <u>cold in the trucks.</u>
> *It's fun working* for him.
> *It was a pleasure to be* there.
> *It's strange that* it hasn't been noticed before.

5 You use 'it' followed by a verb such as 'interest', 'please', 'surprise', or 'upset' which indicates someone's reaction to a fact, situation, or event. The verb is followed by a noun group, and a 'that'-clause or a 'to'-infinitive clause.

> <u>*It pleases me that*</u> he should want to talk about his work.
> <u>*It surprised him to realize*</u> that he hadn't thought about them until now.

6 You can also use 'it' with the passive of a reporting verb and a 'that'-clause when you want to suggest that an opinion or belief is shared by many people. This use is particularly common in news reports, for example in newspapers, on the radio, or on television.

> <u>*It was said that*</u> he could speak their language.
> Nowadays <u>*it is believed that*</u> the size is unimportant.
> <u>*It is thought that*</u> about a million puppies are born each year.

Impersonal subject 'it'

Note that the passive of reporting verbs can also be used without impersonal 'it' to express general opinions.

> _The factories were said to be_ much worse.
> _They are believed to be_ dangerous.

▶ See Units 76 and 77 for more information on reporting verbs.

Impersonal subject 'there'

Main points

You use 'there' followed by a form of 'be' and a noun group to introduce new information.

You use 'there' with a singular or plural verb, depending on whether the following noun is singular or plural.

You can also use 'there' with modals.

---

1 'There' is often an adverb of place.

> *Are you comfortable <u>there?</u>*
> *The book is <u>there</u> on the table.*

You can also use 'there' as the impersonal subject of a sentence when it does not refer to a place. In this case you use 'there' to introduce new information and to focus upon it. After 'there' you use a form of 'be' and a noun group.

> *<u>There is work</u> to be done.*
> *<u>There will be a party</u> tonight.*
> *<u>There was no damage.</u>*
> *<u>There have been two telephone calls.</u>*

Note that the impersonal subject 'there' is often

Impersonal subject 'there'

pronounced without stress, whereas the adverb is almost always stressed.

2 You use 'there' as the impersonal subject to talk about:
● the existence or presence of someone or something

> *There are two people who might know what happened.*
> *There are many possibilities.*
> *There is plenty of bread.*

● something that happens

> *There was a general election that year.*
> *There's a meeting every week.*
> *There was a fierce battle.*

● a number or amount

> *There are forty of us, I think.*
> *There is a great deal of anger about his decision.*
> *There were a lot of people camped there.*

3 When the noun group after the verb is plural, you use a plural verb.

> <u>*There are many reasons*</u> *for this.*
> <u>*There were two men*</u> *in the room.*

Impersonal subject 'there'

You also use a plural verb before phrases such as 'a number (of)', 'a lot (of)', and 'a few (of)'.

> _There were a lot of_ people camped there.
> _There are_ only _a few_ left.

4 When the noun group after the verb is singular or uncountable, you use a singular verb.

> _There is one point_ we must add here.
> _There isn't enough room_ in here.

You also use a singular verb when you are mentioning more than one person or thing and the first noun after the verb is singular or uncountable.

> _There was a man_ and a woman.
> _There was a sofa_ and two chairs.

5 You can also use 'there' with a modal, followed by 'be' or 'have been'.

> _There could be_ a problem.
> _There should be_ a change in government.
> _There can't have been_ anybody outside.
> _There must have been_ some mistake.

6 In spoken and informal written English, short forms of 'be' or a modal are normally used after 'there'.

> _There's_ no danger.
> _There'll_ always _be_ a future for music.
> I knew _there'd be_ trouble.

Impersonal subject 'there'

> *There's been* quite a lot of research into it.
> I didn't even know *there'd been* a murder.

7 You can also use 'there' with 'appear' or 'seem', followed by 'to be' or 'to have been'.

> *There appears to be* a vast amount of confusion
> on this point.
> *There don't seem to be* many people on
> campus.
> *There seems to have been* some carelessness.

Demonstrative pronouns

Main points

You use the demonstrative pronouns 'this', 'that', 'these', and 'those' when you are pointing to physical objects or identifying people.

You use 'one' or 'ones' instead of a noun that has been mentioned or is known.

1 You use the demonstrative pronouns 'this', 'that', 'these', and 'those' when you are pointing to physical objects. 'This' and 'these' refer to things near you, 'that' and 'those' refer to things farther away.

> _This_ is a list of rules.
> 'I brought you _these_'. Adam held out a bag of grapes.
> _That_ looks interesting.
> _Those_ are mine.

You can also use 'this', 'that', 'these', and 'those' as determiners in front of nouns.
➤ See Unit 23.

> _This book_ was a present from my mother.
> When did you buy _that hat?_

Demonstrative pronouns

2 You use 'this', 'that', 'these', and 'those' when you are identifying or introducing people, or asking who they are.

> *Who's <u>this?</u>*
> *<u>These</u> are my children, Susan and Paul.*
> *Was <u>that</u> Patrick on the phone?*

3 You use 'this', 'that', 'these', and 'those' to refer back to things that have already been mentioned.

> *<u>That</u> was an interesting word you used just now.*
> *More money is being pumped into the education system, and we assume <u>this</u> will continue.*
> *'Let's go to the cinema.' – '<u>That</u>'s a good idea.'*
> *<u>These</u> are not easy questions to answer.*

You also use 'this' and 'these' to refer forward to things you are going to mention.

> *<u>This</u> is what I want to say: it wasn't my idea.*
> *<u>These</u> are the topics we will be looking at next week: how the accident happened, whether it could have been avoided, and who was to blame.*
> *<u>This</u> is the important point: you must never see her again.*

Demonstrative pronouns

4 You use 'one' or 'ones' instead of a noun that has already been mentioned or is known in the situation, usually when you are adding information or contrasting two things of the same kind.

> *My car* is *the blue one.*
> *Don't you have* <u>one</u> *with buttons instead of a zip?*
> *Are* <u>the new curtains</u> *longer than* <u>the old ones?</u>

You can use 'which one' or 'which ones' in questions.

> <u>Which one</u> *do you prefer?*
> <u>Which ones</u> *were damaged?*

You can say 'this one', 'that one', 'these ones', and 'those ones'.

> *I like* <u>this one</u> *better.*
> *We'll have* <u>those ones,</u> *thank you.*

You can use 'each one' or 'one each', but note that there is a difference in meaning. In the following examples, 'each one' means 'each brother' but 'one each' means 'one for each child'.

> *I've got three brothers and* <u>each one</u> *lives in a different country.*
> *I bought the children* <u>one each.</u>

Demonstrative pronouns

5 In formal English, people sometimes use 'one' to refer to people in general.

> *One has to think of the practical side of things.*
> *One never knows what to say in such situations.*

6 There are several other types of pronoun, which are dealt with in other units.

➤ See Unit 22 for information on possessive pronouns.

➤ See Unit 6 for information on 'who', 'whom', 'whose', 'which', and 'what' as interrogative pronouns.

➤ See Units 92 and 93 for information on 'that', 'which', 'who', 'whom', and 'whose' as relative pronouns.

Most determiners, except 'the', 'a', 'an', 'every', 'no', and the possessives, are also pronouns.

➤ See Units 27 to 30.

Main points

Reflexive pronouns can be direct or indirect objects.

Most transitive verbs can take a reflexive pronoun as object.

Reflexive pronouns can be the object of a preposition.

Reflexive pronouns can emphasize a noun or pronoun.

1 The reflexive pronouns are:

singular:	myself	yourself	himself
	herself	itself	
plural:	ourselves	yourselves	themselves

Note that, unlike 'you' and 'your', there are two forms for the second person: 'yourself' in the singular and 'yourselves' in the plural.

2 You use reflexive pronouns as the direct or indirect object of the verb when you want to say that the object is the same person or thing as the subject of the verb in the same clause.

Reflexive pronouns

For example, 'John taught himself' means that John did the teaching and was also the person who was taught, and 'Ann poured herself a drink' means that Ann did the pouring and was also the person that the drink was poured for.

> *She* stretched *herself* out on the sofa.
> *The men* formed *themselves* into a line.
> *He* should give *himself* more time.

Note that although the subject 'you' is omitted in imperatives, you can still use 'yourself' or 'yourselves'.

> *Here's the money, go and buy <u>yourself</u> an ice cream.*

3 Most transitive verbs can take a reflexive pronoun.

> *I <u>blame myself</u> for not paying attention.*
> *He <u>introduced himself</u> to me.*

⊖ WARNING: Verbs which describe actions that people normally do to themselves do not take reflexive pronouns in English, although they do in some other languages.

> *I usually <u>shave</u> before breakfast.*
> *She <u>washed</u> very quickly and rushed downstairs.*

▶ See Unit 53 for more information.

Reflexive pronouns

4 You use a reflexive pronoun as the object of a preposition when the object of the preposition refers to the same person or thing as the subject of the verb in the same clause.

> *I was thoroughly ashamed <u>of myself.</u>*
> *They are making fools <u>of themselves.</u>*
> *Tell me <u>about yourself.</u>*

Note that you use personal pronouns, not reflexive pronouns, when referring to places and after 'with' meaning 'accompanied by'.

> *<u>You</u> should have your notes <u>in front of you.</u>*
> *<u>He</u> would have to bring Judy <u>with him.</u>*

5 You use reflexive pronouns after nouns or pronouns to emphasize the person or thing that you are referring to.

> *<u>The town itself</u> was so small that it didn't have a bank.*
> *<u>I myself</u> have never read the book.*

6 You use a reflexive pronoun at the end of a clause to emphasize that someone did something without any help from anyone else.

> *She had printed the card <u>herself</u>.*
> *I'll take it down to the police station <u>myself</u>.*
> *Did you make these <u>yourself?</u>*

Reflexive pronouns

7 You use reflexive pronouns with 'by' to say:

● that someone does something without any help from other people

> …*when babies start eating their meals <u>by themselves.</u>*
> *She was certain she could manage <u>by herself.</u>*

● that someone is alone

> *He went off to sit by <u>himself.</u>*
> *I was there for about six months by <u>myself.</u>*

You can also use 'on my own', 'on your own', and so on, to say that someone is alone or does something without any help.

> *We were in the park <u>on our own.</u>*
> *They managed to reach the village <u>on their own.</u>*

You can use 'all' for emphasis.

> *Did you put those shelves up <u>all by yourself?</u>*
> *We can't solve this problem <u>all on our own.</u>*

⊖ WARNING: 'One another' and 'each other' are not reflexive pronouns.

➤ See Unit 54 for more information on 'one another' and 'each other'.

89

Indefinite pronouns

Main points

Indefinite pronouns refer to people or things without saying exactly who or what they are.

When an indefinite pronoun is the subject, it always takes a singular verb.

You often use a plural pronoun to refer back to an indefinite pronoun.

---

1 The indefinite pronouns are:

anybody	everybody	nobody	somebody
anyone	everyone	no one	someone
anything	everything	nothing	something

Note that 'no one' is written as two words, or sometimes with a hyphen: 'no-one'.

2 You use indefinite pronouns when you want to refer to people or things without saying exactly who or what they are. The pronouns ending in '-body' and '-one' refer to people, and those ending in '-thing' refer to things.

Indefinite pronouns

> *I was there for over an hour before <u>anybody</u> came.*
> *It had to be <u>someone</u> with a car.*
> *Jane said <u>nothing</u> for a moment.*

3 When an indefinite pronoun is the subject, it always takes a singular verb, even when it refers to more than one person or thing.

> <u>*Everyone knows*</u> *that.*
> <u>*Everything was*</u> *fine.*
> <u>*Is anybody*</u> *there?*

When you refer back to indefinite pronouns, you use plural pronouns or possessives, and a plural verb.

> *Ask <u>anyone</u>. <u>They</u>'ll tell you.*
> *Has <u>everyone</u> eaten as much as <u>they</u> want?*
> *You can't tell <u>somebody</u> why <u>they</u>'ve failed.*

● WARNING: Some speakers prefer to use singular pronouns. They prefer to say 'You can't tell somebody why he or she has failed'.

4 You can add apostrophe s ('s) to indefinite pronouns that refer to people.

> *She was given a room in <u>someone's</u> studio.*
> *That was <u>nobody's</u> business but mine.*

Indefinite pronouns

⊖ WARNING: You do not usually add apostrophe s ('s) to indefinite pronouns that refer to things. You do not say 'something's value', you say 'the value of something'.

5 You use indefinite pronouns beginning with 'some-' in:

● affirmative clauses

> _Somebody_ shouted.
> I want to introduce you to _someone._

● questions expecting the answer 'yes'

> Would you like _something_ to drink?
> Can you get _someone_ to do it?

6 You use indefinite pronouns beginning with 'any-':

● as the subject or object in statements

> _Anyone_ knows that you need a licence.
> You still haven't told me _anything._

You do not use them as the subject of a negative statement. You do not say 'Anybody can't come in'.

● in both affirmative and negative questions

> Does _anybody_ agree with me?
> Won't _anyone_ help me?

Indefinite pronouns

7 If you use an indefinite pronoun beginning with 'no-', you must not use another negative word in the same clause. You do not say 'There wasn't nothing'.

> *There was <u>nothing</u> you could do.*
> *<u>Nobody</u> left, <u>nobody</u> went away.*

8 You use the indefinite adverbs 'anywhere', 'everywhere', 'nowhere', and 'somewhere' to talk about places in a general way. 'Nowhere' makes a clause negative.

> *I thought I'd seen you <u>somewhere.</u>*
> *No-one can find Howard or Barbara <u>anywhere.</u>*
> *There was <u>nowhere</u> to hide.*

9 You can use 'else' after indefinite pronouns and adverbs to refer to people, things, or places other than those that have been mentioned.

> *<u>Everyone else</u> is downstairs.*
> *I don't like it here. Let's go <u>somewhere else.</u>*

Possession

Main points

Possessives and possessive pronouns are used to say that one person or thing belongs to another or is connected with another.

You use apostrophe s ('s) to say who something belongs to.

You use phrases with 'of' to say that one person or thing belongs to another or is connected with another.

[1] You use possessives to say that a person or thing belongs to another person or thing or is connected with them. The possessives are sometimes called 'possessive adjectives'.

| my | your | his | her | its | our | their |

Note that 'your' is both singular and plural.

> *I'd been waiting a long time to park <u>my car</u>.*
> *They took off <u>their shoes</u>.*

⊖ WARNING: The possessive 'its' is not spelled with an apostrophe. The form 'it's' with an apostrophe is the short form for 'it is' or 'it has'.

Possession

2 You put numbers and adjectives after the possessive and in front of the noun.

> *Their two small children were playing outside.*
> *She got a bicycle on her sixth birthday.*

3 You use a possessive pronoun when you want to refer to a person or thing and to say who that person or thing belongs to or is connected with. The possessive pronouns are:

mine	yours	his	hers	ours	theirs

Note that 'yours' is both singular and plural.

> *Is that coffee yours or mine ?*
> *It was his fault, not theirs.*

● WARNING: There is no possessive pronoun 'its'.

4 You can also say who or what something belongs to or is connected with by using a noun with apostrophe s ('s). For example, if John owns a motorbike, you can refer to it as 'John's motorbike'.

> *Sylvia put her hand on John's arm.*
> *I like the car's design.*

You add apostrophe s ('s) to singular nouns and irregular plural nouns, usually referring to people rather than things.

Possession

I wore a pair of my <u>sister's</u> boots.
<u>Children's</u> birthday parties can be boring.

With plural nouns ending in '-s' you only add the apostrophe (').

It is not his <u>parents'</u> problem.

You add apostrophe s ('s) to people's names, even when they end in '-s'.

Could you give me <u>Charles's</u> address?

Note that when you use two or more names linked by 'and', you put the apostrophe s ('s) after the last name.

They have bought <u>Sue and Tim's</u> car.

5 When you want to refer to someone's home, or to some common shops and places of work, you can use apostrophe s ('s) after a name or noun on its own.

He's round at <u>David's.</u>
He bought it at the <u>chemist's.</u>
She must go to the <u>doctor's.</u>

6 You can also use apostrophe s ('s) with some expressions of time to identify something, or to say how much time is involved.

Possession

Did you see the cartoon in <u>yesterday's</u> news-paper?
They have four <u>weeks'</u> holiday per year.

7 | You can use a prepositional phrase beginning with 'of' to say that one person or thing belongs to or is connected with another.

She is the mother <u>of the boy</u> who lives next door.
Ellen aimlessly turned the pages <u>of her magazine.</u>

After 'of' you can use a possessive pronoun, or a noun or name with apostrophe s ('s).

He was an old friend <u>of mine.</u>
That word was a favourite <u>of your father's.</u>
She's a friend <u>of Stephen's.</u>

8 | You can add 'own' after a possessive, or a noun or name with apostrophe s ('s), for emphasis.

<u>My own</u> view is that there are no serious problems.
The <u>professor's own</u> answer may be unacceptable.

Determiners

Main points

Determiners are used at the beginning of noun groups.

You use specific determiners when people know exactly which things or people you are talking about.

You use general determiners to talk about people or things without saying exactly who or what they are.

1 When you use a determiner, you put it at the beginning of a noun group, in front of numbers or adjectives.

> I met _the two Swedish girls_ in London.
> _Our main bedroom_ is through there.
> Have you got _another red card?_

2 When the people or things that you are talking about have already been mentioned, or the people you are talking to know exactly which ones you mean, you use a specific determiner.

> _The_ man began to run towards _the_ boy.
> Young people don't like _these_ operas.
> _Her_ face was very red.

Determiners

The specific determiners are:

the definite article:	the
demonstratives:	this that these those
possessives:	my your his her its our their

Note that 'your' is used both for the singular and plural possessive.

▶ See Unit 19 for 'this', 'that', 'these', and 'those' as pronouns.

3 When you are mentioning people or things for the first time, or talking about them generally without saying exactly which ones you mean, you use a general determiner.

> *There was a man in the lift.*
> *We went to an art exhibition.*
> *You can stop at any time you like.*
> *There were several reasons for this.*

The general determiners are:

a	all	an	another
any	both	each	either
enough	every	few	fewer
less	little	many	more
most	much	neither	no
other	several	some	

Determiners

4 Each general determiner is used with particular types of noun, such as:

● singular count nouns

a	an	another	any	each
either	every	neither	no	

> I got <u>a postcard</u> from Susan.
> He opened <u>another shop</u>.
> <u>Any big tin container</u> will do.

● plural count nouns

all	any	both	enough
few	fewer	many	more
most	no	other	several
some			

> There were <u>few doctors</u> available.
> <u>Several projects</u> were postponed.
> He spoke <u>many different languages.</u>

● uncount nouns

all	any	enough	less	little	more
most	much	no	some		

> There was <u>little applause.</u>
> He did not speak <u>much English.</u>
> We need <u>more information.</u>

Determiners

⊖ WARNING: The following general determiners can never be used with uncount nouns.

a	an	another	both	each
either	every	few	many	neither
several				

5. Most of the determiners are also pronouns, except 'the', 'a', 'an', 'every', 'no' and the possessives.

> *I saw <u>several</u> in the woods last night.*
> *There is <u>enough</u> for all of us.*
> *Have you got <u>any</u> that I could borrow?*

You use 'one' as a pronoun instead of 'a' or 'an', 'none' instead of 'no', and 'each' instead of 'every'.

> *Have you got <u>one?</u>*
> *There are <u>none</u> left.*
> *<u>Each</u> has a separate box and number.*

Main uses of 'the'

Main points

You can use 'the' in front of any noun.

You use 'the' when the person you are talking to knows which person or thing you mean.

You use 'the' when you are referring back to someone or something.

You use 'the' when you are specifying which person or thing you are talking about.

You use 'the' when you are referring to something that is unique.

You use 'the' when you want to use one thing as an example to say something about all things of the same type.

1. 'The' is called the definite article, and is the commonest determiner. You use 'the' when the person you are talking to knows which person or thing you mean. You can use 'the' in front of any noun, whether it is a singular count noun, an uncount noun, or a plural count noun.

> She dropped _the can._

Main uses of 'the'

I remembered <u>the fun</u> I had with them last summer.
<u>The girls</u> were not at home.

2 You use 'the' with a noun when you are referring back to someone or something that has already been mentioned.

I called for <u>a waiter</u> … … <u>The waiter</u> with a moustache came.
I have bought <u>a house</u> in Wales… … <u>The house</u> is in an agricultural area.

3 You use 'the' with a noun and a qualifier, such as a prepositional phrase or a relative clause, when you are specifying which person or thing you are talking about.

I've no idea about <u>the geography of Great Britain.</u>
<u>The book that I recommended</u> now costs over three pounds.

4 You use 'the' with a noun when you are referring to something of which there is only one in the world.

They all sat in <u>the sun.</u>
We have landed men on <u>the moon.</u>
<u>The sky</u> was a brilliant blue.

You also use 'the' when you are referring to something of which there is only one in a particular place.

> *Mrs Robertson heard that <u>the church</u> had been bombed.*
> *He decided to put some words on <u>the blackboard.</u>*

5 You can use 'the' with a singular count noun when you want to make a general statement about all things of that type. For example, if you say 'The whale is the largest mammal in the world', you are talking about all whales, not one particular whale.

> *<u>The computer</u> allows us to deal with a lot of data very quickly.*
> *My father's favourite flower is <u>the rose.</u>*

6 You can use 'the' with a singular count noun when you are referring to a system or service. For example, you can use 'the phone' to refer to a telephone system and 'the bus' to refer to a bus service.

> *I don't like using <u>the phone.</u>*
> *How long does it take to get to London on <u>the train?</u>*

Main uses of 'the'

7 You can use 'the' with the name of a musical instrument when you are talking about someone's ability to play the instrument.

> 'You play <u>the guitar,</u> I see,' said Simon.
> Geoff plays <u>the piano</u> very well.

Other uses of 'the'

Main points

You do not normally use 'the' with proper nouns referring to people. You do use 'the' with many proper nouns referring to geographical places.

You use 'the' with some adjectives to talk about groups of people.

---

1 You do not normally use 'the' with proper nouns that are people's names. However, if you are talking about a family, you can say 'the Browns'.
You use 'the' with some titles, such as 'the Queen of England', and with the names of some organizations, buildings, newspapers, and works of art.

> ... _the_ United Nations...   ... _the_ Taj Mahal.
> ... _the_ Times...   ... _the_ Mona Lisa.

2 You do use 'the' with some proper nouns referring to geographical places.

> ... _the_ Bay of Biscay...   ... _the_ Suez Canal.
> ... _the_ Arabian Gulf...   ... _the_ Pacific Ocean.

You use 'the' with countries whose names include

Other uses of 'the'

words such as 'kingdom', 'republic', 'states', or 'union'.

> ... _the_ United Kingdom...   ... _the_ Czech Republic.

You use 'the' with countries that have plural nouns as their names.

> ... _the_ Netherlands...   ... _the_ Philippines.

Note that you do not use 'the' with countries that have singular nouns as their names, such as 'China', 'Italy', or 'Turkey'.

You use 'the' with names of mountain ranges and groups of islands.

> ... _the_ Alps...   ... _the_ Himalayas.
> ... _the_ Bahamas...   ... _the_ Canaries.

Note that you do not use 'the' with the names of individual mountains such as 'Everest' or 'Etna', or the names of individual islands such as 'Sicily', 'Minorca', or 'Bali'.

You use 'the' with regions of the world, or regions of a country that include 'north', 'south', 'east', or 'west'.

> ... _the_ Middle East...   ... _the_ west of Ireland.
> ... _the_ north of England...   ... _the_ Far East.

Note that there are some exceptions.

> ...North America...   ...South-East Asia.

Other uses of 'the'

You do not use 'the' with 'northern', 'southern', 'eastern', or 'western' and a singular name.

> … _northern_ England…   … _western_ Africa.

You use 'the' with the names of areas of water such as seas, oceans, rivers, canals, gulfs, and straits.

> … _the_ Mediterranean Sea.
> … _the_ Atlantic Ocean.
> … _the_ river Ganges.
> … _the_ Panama Canal.
> … _the_ Gulf of Mexico.
> … _the_ straits of Gibraltar.

Note that you do not use 'the' with lakes.

> …Lake Geneva…   …Lake Superior.

Note that you do not use 'the' with continents, cities, streets, or addresses.

> …Asia…   …Tokyo…   …Oxford Street…
> …15 Park Street.

3 You use 'the' with adjectives such as 'rich', 'poor', 'young', 'old', and 'unemployed' to talk about a general group of people. You do not need a noun.

> Only _the rich_ could afford his firm's products.
> They were discussing the problem of _the unemployed._

Other uses of 'the'

When you use 'the' with an adjective as the subject of a verb, you use a plural verb.

> In the cities *the poor are* as badly off as they were in the villages.

4 You use 'the' with some nationality adjectives to talk about the people who live in a country.

> *They will be increasingly dependent on the support of the French.*
> *The Spanish claimed that the money had not been paid.*

With other nationalities, you use a plural noun.

> *…Germans…*   *…the Americans.*

When you use 'the' with a nationality adjective as the subject of a verb, you use a plural verb.

> *The British are worried.*

5 You use 'the' with superlatives.

> *He was the cleverest man I ever knew.*
> *He was the youngest.*
> *His shoulders hurt the worst.*
> *It was the most exciting summer of their lives.*

'A' and 'an'

Main points

You only use 'a' or 'an' with singular count nouns.

You use 'a' or 'an' to talk about a person or thing for the first time.

1 You only use 'a' or 'an' with singular count nouns. 'A' and 'an' are called the indefinite article.

> *I got <u>a postcard</u> from Susan.*
> *He was eating <u>an apple.</u>*

Remember that you use 'a' in front of a word that begins with a consonant sound even if the first letter is a vowel, for example 'a piece, a university, a European language'. You use 'an' in front of a word that begins with a vowel sound even if the first letter is a consonant, for example 'an exercise, an idea, an honest man'.

2 You use 'a' or 'an' when you are talking about a person or thing for the first time.

> *She picked up <u>a book.</u>*

'A' and 'an'

After weeks of looking, we eventually bought a house.
A colleague and I got some money to do research on rats.

Note that the second time you refer to the same person or thing, you use 'the'.

She picked up a book … … The book was lying on the table.
After weeks of looking, we bought a house …
… The house was in a village.

3 After the verb 'be' or another link verb, you can use 'a' or 'an' with an adjective and a noun to give more information about someone or something.

His brother was a sensitive child.
He seemed a worried man.
It was a really beautiful house.

You can also use 'a' or 'an' with a noun followed by a qualifier, such as a prepositional phrase or a relative clause, when you want to give more information about someone or something.

The information was contained in an article on biology.
I chose a picture that reminded me of my own country.

'A' and 'an'

4 You use 'a' or 'an' after the verb 'be' or another link verb when you are saying what someone is or what job they have.

> *He became a school teacher.*
> *She is a model and an artist.*

5 You use 'a' or 'an' to mean 'one' with some numbers. You can use 'a' or 'an' with nouns that refer to whole numbers, fractions, money, weights, or measures.

a hundred	a quarter	a pound	a kilo
a thousand	a half	a dollar	a litre

6 You do not use 'a' or 'an' with uncount nouns or plural count nouns. You do not need to use a determiner at all with plural count nouns, but you can use the determiners 'any', 'a few', 'many', 'several', or 'some'.

> *I love dogs.*
> *Do you have any dogs?*
> *Many adults don't listen to children.*
> *I have some children like that in my class.*

Note that if you do not use a determiner with a plural count noun, you are often making a general statement about people or things of that type. For example, if you say 'I love dogs', you mean all dogs. However, if you say 'There are eggs in the kitchen', you mean there are some eggs. If you do use a

'A' and 'an'

determiner, you mean a number of people or things but not all of them, without saying exactly how many.

> *I have <u>some friends</u> coming for dinner.*
> *He has bought <u>some plants</u> for the house.*
> *I have <u>some important things</u> to tell them.*

All, most, no, none

Main points

You use 'all' with plural count nouns and uncount nouns. You use 'all' to talk about every person or thing in the world, or in the group you are talking about.

You use 'most' with plural count nouns and uncount nouns. You use 'most' to talk about nearly all of a number of people or things, or nearly all of a quantity of something.

You use 'no' with singular and plural count nouns and uncount nouns. You use 'no' to say that something does not exist or is not present.

1 You use 'all' with plural count nouns and uncount nouns to talk about every person or thing in the world or in the group that you are talking about.

> _All children_ should complete the primary course.
> _All important decisions_ were taken by the government.
> He soon lost _all hope_ of becoming a rock star.
> _All luggage_ will be searched.

All, most, no, none

2 You use 'most' with plural count nouns and uncount nouns to talk about nearly all of a number of people or things, or nearly all of a quantity of something.

> *The method was suitable for <u>most purposes.</u>*
> *<u>Most good drivers</u> stop at zebra crossings.*
> *<u>Most milk</u> is still delivered to people's houses.*
> *He ignored <u>most advice,</u> and did what he thought best.*

3 You use 'no' with singular count nouns, plural count nouns, and uncount nouns to say that something does not exist or is not present.

> *There was <u>no chair</u> for me to sit on.*
> *They had <u>no immediate plans</u> to change house.*
> *<u>No money</u> was available for the operation.*

Note that if there is another word in the clause that makes it negative, you use 'any', not 'no'.

> *It has<u>n't</u> made <u>any difference.</u>*
> *He will <u>never</u> do <u>any work</u> for me again.*

4 'All' and 'most' are also pronouns, so you can say 'all of' and 'most of'. 'No' is not a pronoun, so you must say 'none of'.

> *He spent <u>all of the money</u> on a new car.*
> *<u>Most of my friends</u> live in London.*
> *<u>None of those farmers</u> had ever driven a tractor.*

All, most, no, none

Note that you use 'all of', 'most of', and 'none of' with an object pronoun.

> _All of us_ were sleeping.
> I had seen _most of them_ before.
> _None of them_ came to the party.

Note that if the clause is already negative, you use 'any of', not 'none of'.

> I had<u>n't</u> eaten <u>any of</u> the biscuits.

When 'none of' is followed by a plural noun or pronoun, the verb is usually plural, but can be singular.

> _None of us are_ the same.
> _None of them has_ lasted very long.

5 You can use 'all the' with a plural count noun or an uncount noun. There is no difference in meaning between 'all the' and 'all of the'.

> _All the girls_ think it's great.
> _All the best jokes_ came at the end of the programme.
> Thank you for _all the help_ you gave me.

⊖ WARNING: You cannot say 'most the' or 'none the'. You must say 'most of the' or 'none of the'.

6 You can use 'all' after a noun or pronoun to emphasize that the noun or pronoun refers to everyone

116

All, most, no, none

or everything that has been mentioned or is involved.

Note that you can use 'all' to emphasize the subject or the object.

> *The band all live together in the same house.*
> *I enjoyed it all.*

Both, either, neither

Main points

You use 'both', 'either', and 'neither' to talk about two people or things that have been mentioned or are known to the hearer.

You use 'both' with plural nouns, and 'either' and 'neither' with singular nouns.

You use 'both of', 'either of', and 'neither of' with plural nouns or pronouns.

1 You use 'both', 'either', and 'neither' when you are saying something about two people or things that have been mentioned, or are known to the person you are talking to.

> *There were excellent performances from <u>both actresses.</u>*
> *Denis held his cocoa in <u>both hands.</u>*
> *No argument could move <u>either man</u> from this decision.*
> *<u>Neither report</u> mentioned the Americans.*

2 You use 'both' when you think of the two people or things as a group. You use 'both' with a plural noun.

Both, either, neither

Both children were happy with their presents.
Both policies make good sense.

3 You use 'either' when you think of the two people
or things as individuals. You use 'either' with a singular noun.

Either way is acceptable.
She could not see *either man.*

4 You use 'neither' when you are thinking of the two
people or things as individuals and you are making a negative statement about them. You use 'neither' with a singular noun.

In reality, *neither party* was enthusiastic.
Neither man knew what he was doing.

5 You can use 'both' with a specific determiner such
as 'the', 'these', or 'my'.

Both the young men agreed to come.
Both these books have been recommended
to us.
Both her parents were dead.

⊖ WARNING: You cannot use 'either' or 'neither'
with a specific determiner.

6 You can use 'both of', 'either of', or 'neither of' with
a plural noun or pronoun.

119

Both, either, neither

Note that when 'both of', 'either of', and 'neither of' are followed by a noun rather than a pronoun, you must use a specific determiner such as 'the', 'these', or 'her' before the noun.

> _Both of these restaurants_ are excellent.
> _Either of them_ could have done the job.
> _Neither of our boys_ was involved.

Note that 'neither of' is normally used with a singular verb but it can be used with a plural verb.

> _Neither of us <u>was having</u> any luck._
> _Neither of the children <u>were</u> there._

7 | Remember that you can also use 'both', 'either', and 'neither' as conjunctions. You use 'both...and' to give two alternatives and say that each of them is possible or true.

> _I am looking for opportunities <u>both</u> in this country <u>and</u> abroad._
> _<u>Both</u> I <u>and</u> my wife were surprised to see you there._

You use 'either...or' to give two alternatives and say that only one of them is possible or true.

> _You can have <u>either</u> fruit <u>or</u> ice cream._
> _I was expecting you <u>either</u> today <u>or</u> tomorrow._
> _You <u>either</u> love him <u>or</u> hate him._

Both, either, neither

You also use 'neither...nor' to give two alternatives and say that each of them is not possible or is not true.

> *Neither Margaret nor John was there.*
> *He did it neither quickly nor well.*

Quantity 1

Main points

You use 'much' and 'little' with uncount nouns to talk about a quantity of something.

You use 'many' and 'few' with plural nouns to talk about a number of people or things.

You use 'much' in negative sentences and questions, and 'a lot of' or 'plenty of' rather than 'much' in affirmative sentences.

You use 'more' and 'less' with uncount nouns, and 'more' and 'fewer' with plural count nouns.

1 You use 'much' to talk about a large quantity of something, and 'little' to talk about a small quantity of something. You only use 'much' and 'little' with uncount nouns.

> I haven't got <u>much time.</u>
> We've made <u>little progress.</u>

2 You use 'many' to talk about a large number of people or things, and 'few' to talk about a small number of people or things. You can only use 'many' and 'few' with plural count nouns.

Quantity 1

He wrote <u>many novels.</u>
There were <u>few visitors</u> to our house.

3 You normally use 'much' in negative sentences and questions.

He did <u>not</u> speak <u>much</u> English.
Why have<u>n't</u> I given <u>much</u> attention to this problem?

In affirmative sentences you do not use 'much', you use 'a lot of', 'lots of', or 'plenty of' instead. You can use them with both uncount nouns and plural nouns.

He demanded <u>a lot of attention.</u>
I make <u>a lot of mistakes.</u>
They spent <u>lots of time</u> on the project.
He remembered a large room with <u>lots of windows.</u>
I've got <u>plenty of money.</u>
There are always <u>plenty of jobs</u> to be done.

Note that you can use 'so much' and 'too much' in affirmative sentences.

She spends <u>so much time</u> here.
There is <u>too much chance</u> of error.

4 You use 'so much' to emphasize that a large quantity of something is involved.

123

Quantity 1

I have <u>so much work</u> to do.
They have <u>so much money</u> and we have so little.

You use 'too much' and 'too many' to say that the quantity of something, or the number of people or things, is larger than is reasonable or necessary.

He has <u>too much work</u>.
<u>Too many people</u> still smoke.

You use 'very many' to emphasize that a large number of people or things are involved.

<u>Very many old people</u> live alone.

Note that 'very much' is used with nouns and verbs.

There isn't <u>very much time</u>.
I <u>liked</u> it <u>very much</u>.

5 You use 'few' and 'little' to emphasize that only a small quantity of something or a small number of people or things are involved. They can be used with 'very' for greater emphasis.

The town has <u>few monuments.</u>
I have <u>little time</u> for anything but work.
<u>Very few cars</u> had reversing lights.
I had <u>very little money</u> left.

Note that 'a few' and 'a little' just indicate that a quantity or number is small.

Quantity 1

He spread <u>a little honey</u> on a slice of bread.
I usually do <u>a few jobs</u> for him in the house.

6 You use 'more' with uncount nouns and plural count nouns to refer to a quantity of something or a number of people or things that is greater than another quantity or number.

> *His visit might do <u>more harm</u> than good.*
> *He does <u>more hours</u> than I do.*

You use 'less' with uncount nouns to refer to an amount of something that is smaller than another amount.

> *The poor have <u>less access</u> to education.*
> *This machinery uses <u>less energy.</u>*

You use 'fewer', or 'less' in informal English, with plural nouns to refer to a number of people or things that is smaller than another number.

> *There are <u>fewer trees</u> here.*
> *They have sold <u>less computers</u> this year.*

Quantity 2

Main points

You use 'some' to talk about a quantity or number without being precise.

You use 'any' to talk about a quantity or number that may or may not exist.

You use 'another', or 'another' and a number, to talk about additional people or things.

You use 'each' and 'every' to talk about all the members of a group of people or things.

1. You use 'some' with uncount nouns and plural nouns to talk about a quantity of something or a number of people or things without being precise.

> *I have left <u>some food</u> for you in the fridge.*
> *<u>Some trains</u> are running late.*

You normally use 'some' in affirmative sentences.

> *There's <u>some chocolate cake</u> over there.*
> *I had <u>some good ideas.</u>*

You use 'some' in questions when you expect the answer to be 'yes', for example in offers or requests.

> *Would you like <u>some coffee?</u>*
> *Could you give me <u>some examples?</u>*

Quantity 2

You can use 'some' with a singular noun when you do not know which person or thing is involved, or you think it does not matter.

> *Some man phoned, but didn't leave his number.*
> *Is there some problem?*

2 You use 'any' in front of plural and uncount nouns to talk about a quantity of something that may or may not exist. You normally use 'any' in questions and negative sentences.

> *Are there any jobs men can do but women can't?*
> *It hasn't made any difference.*

You use 'any' with a singular noun to emphasize that it does not matter which person or thing is involved.

> *Any container will do.*

You can use 'no' with an affirmative verb instead of 'not any'.

> *There weren't any tomatoes left.*
> *There were no tomatoes left.*

You can also use 'not' and 'any', or 'no', with a comparative.

> *Her house wasn't any better than ours.*
> *Her house was no better than ours.*

Quantity 2

3 You use 'another' with singular nouns to talk about an additional person or thing.

> *Could I have <u>another cup of coffee</u>?*
> *He opened <u>another shop</u> last month.*

You can also use 'another' with a number and a plural noun to talk about more people or things.

> *<u>Another four years</u> passed before we met again.*
> *I've got <u>another three books</u> to read.*

You use 'other' with plural nouns and 'the other' with singular or plural nouns.

> *I've got <u>other things</u> to think about.*
> *<u>The other</u> man has gone.*
> *<u>The other</u> European countries have all beaten us.*

4 You use 'each' or 'every' with a singular noun to talk about all the members of a group of people or things. You use 'each' when you are thinking about the members as individuals, and 'every' when you are making a general statement about all of them.

> *<u>Each county</u> is subdivided into several districts.*
> *<u>Each applicant</u> has five choices.*
> *<u>Every child</u> would have milk <u>every day</u>.*
> *She spoke to <u>every person</u> at that party.*

Quantity 2

You can modify 'every' but not 'each'.

> *He spoke to them <u>nearly every day.</u>*
> *We went out <u>almost every evening.</u>*

5 You can use 'some of', 'any of', or 'each of', and a noun group to talk about a number of people or things in a group of people or things.

> *<u>Some of the information</u> has already been analysed.*
> *It was more expensive than <u>any of the other magazines.</u>*
> *He gave <u>each of us</u> advice about our present goals.*

You can use 'each of' and a plural noun group but 'every' must be followed by 'one of'.

> *<u>Each of the drawings</u> is different.*
> *<u>Every one of them</u> is given a financial target.*

Note that you can also use 'each' with 'one of'.

> *This view of poverty influences <u>each one of us.</u>*

Position of adjectives

Main points

There are two main positions for adjectives: in front of a noun, or as the complement of a link verb.

Most adjectives can be used in either of these positions, but some adjectives can only be used in one.

1 Most adjectives can be used in a noun group, after determiners and numbers if there are any, in front of the noun.

> He had a <u>beautiful smile.</u>
> She bought a loaf of <u>white bread.</u>
> Six <u>new epiodes</u> will be filmed.
> There was no <u>clear evidence.</u>

2 Most adjectives can also be used after a link verb such as 'be', 'become', or 'feel'.

> I'<u>m cold.</u>
> I <u>felt angry.</u>
> Nobody <u>seemed amused.</u>

Position of adjectives

3 Some adjectives are normally used only after a link verb.

afraid	alive	alone	asleep	aware
content	due	glad	ill	ready
sorry	sure	unable	well	

For example, you can say 'She was glad', but you do not talk about 'a glad woman'.

> I wanted to <u>be alone.</u>
> We were <u>getting ready</u> for bed.
> I<u>'m</u> not quite <u>sure.</u>
> He didn't know whether to <u>feel glad</u> or <u>sorry.</u>

4 Some adjectives are normally used only in front of a noun.

atomic	countless	digital
eastern	existing	indoor
introductory	maximum	neighbouring
northern	occasional	outdoor
southern	western	

For example, you talk about 'an atomic bomb', but you do not say 'The bomb was atomic'.

> He sent <u>countless letters</u> to the newspapers.
> This book includes a good <u>introductory chapter</u> on forests.

5 When you use an adjective to emphasize a strong feeling or opinion, it always comes in front of a noun.

absolute	complete	entire	outright
perfect	positive	pure	real
total	true	utter	

Some of it was <u>absolute rubbish.</u>
He made me feel like a <u>complete idiot.</u>

6 Some adjectives that describe size or age can come after a noun group consisting of a number or determiner and a noun that indicates the unit of measurement.

deep	high	long	old	tall	thick	wide

He was about <u>six feet tall.</u>
The water was <u>several metres deep.</u>
The baby is <u>nine months old.</u>

Note that you do not say 'two pounds heavy', you say 'two pounds in weight'.

7 A few adjectives are used alone after a noun.

designate	elect	galore	incarnate

She was now the <u>president elect.</u>
There are empty <u>houses galore.</u>

Position of adjectives

8 A few adjectives have a different meaning depending on whether they come in front of or after a noun.

concerned	involved	present	proper
responsible			

For example, 'the concerned mother' means a mother who is worried, but 'the mother concerned' means the mother who has been mentioned.

> *It's one of those incredibly <u>involved stories.</u>*
> *The <u>people involved</u> are all doctors.*
> *I'm worried about the <u>present situation.</u>*
> *Of the 18 <u>people present,</u> I knew only one.*
> *Her parents were trying to act in a <u>responsible manner.</u>*
> *We do not know the <u>person responsible</u> for his death.*

Order of adjectives

Main points

You put opinion adjectives in front of descriptive adjectives.

You put general opinion adjectives in front of specific opinion adjectives.

You can sometimes vary the order of adjectives.

If you use two or more descriptive adjectives, you put them in a particular order.

If you use a noun in front of another noun, you put any adjectives in front of the first noun.

1 You often want to add more information to a noun than you can with one adjective. In theory, you can use the adjectives in any order, depending on the quality you want to emphasize. In practice, however, there is a normal order.

When you use two or more adjectives in front of a noun, you usually put an adjective that expresses your opinion in front of an adjective that just describes something.

You live in a <u>nice big</u> house.

Order of adjectives

>*He is a <u>naughty little</u> boy.*
>*She was wearing a <u>beautiful pink</u> suit.*

2. When you use more than one adjective to express your opinion, an adjective with a more general meaning such as 'good', 'bad', 'nice', or 'lovely' usually comes before an adjective with a more specific meaning such as 'comfortable', 'clean', or 'dirty'.

>*I sat in a <u>lovely comfortable</u> armchair in the corner.*
>*He put on a <u>nice clean</u> shirt.*
>*It was a <u>horrible dirty</u> room.*

3. You can use adjectives to describe various qualities of people or things. For example, you might want to indicate their size, their shape, or the country they come from.

Descriptive adjectives belong to six main types, but you are unlikely ever to use all six types in the same noun group. If you did, you would normally put them in the following order:

size age shape colour nationality material

This means that if you want to use an 'age' adjective and a 'nationality' adjective, you put the 'age' adjective first.

>*We met some <u>young Chinese</u> girls.*

Similarly, a 'shape' adjective normally comes before a 'colour' adjective.

> *He had <u>round black</u> eyes.*

Other combinations of adjectives follow the same order.

Note that 'material' means any substance, not only cloth.

> *There was a <u>large round wooden</u> table in the room.*
> *The man was carrying a <u>small black plastic</u> bag.*

4 You usually put comparative and superlative adjectives in front of other adjectives.

> *Some of the <u>better English</u> actors have gone to live in Hollywood.*
> *These are the <u>highest monthly</u> figures on record.*

5 When you use a noun in front of another noun, you never put adjectives between them. You put any adjectives in front of the first noun.

> *He works in the <u>French</u> film industry.*
> *He receives a <u>large weekly</u> cash payment.*

6 When you use two adjectives as the complement of a link verb, you use a conjunction such as 'and'

Order of adjectives

to link them. With three or more adjectives, you link
the last two with a conjunction, and put commas
after the others.

The day was <u>hot and dusty.</u>
The room was <u>large but square.</u>
The house was <u>old, damp and smelly.</u>
We felt <u>hot, tired and thirsty.</u>

Adjective + 'to' or 'that'

Main points

Adjectives used after link verbs are often followed by 'to'-infinitive clauses or 'that'-clauses.

Some adjectives are always followed by 'to'-infinitive clauses.

You often use 'to'-infinitive clauses or 'that'-clauses after adjectives to express feelings or opinions.

You often use 'to'-infinitive clauses after adjectives when the subject is impersonal 'it'.

1 After link verbs, you often use adjectives that describe how someone feels about an action or situation. With some adjectives, you can add a 'to'-infinitive clause or a 'that'-clause to say what the action or situation is.

afraid	anxious	ashamed	disappointed
frightened	glad	happy	pleased
proud	sad	surprised	unhappy

If the subject is the same in both clauses, you usually use a 'to'-infinitive clause. If the subject is different, you must use a 'that'-clause.

Adjective + 'to' or 'that'

I was <u>happy to see</u> them again.
He was <u>happy that</u> they were coming.

You often use a 'to'-infinitive clause when talking about future time in relation to the main clause.

I am <u>afraid to go</u> home.
He was <u>anxious to leave</u> before it got dark.

You often use a 'that'-clause when talking about present or past time in relation to the main clause.

He was <u>anxious that</u> the passport was missing.
They were <u>afraid that</u> I might have talked to the police.

2 You often use 'sorry' with a 'that'-clause. Note that 'that' is often omitted.

I'm very <u>sorry that</u> I can't join you.
I'm <u>sorry</u> I'm so late.

3 Some adjectives are not usually used alone, but have a 'to'-infinitive clause after them to say what action or situation the adjective relates to.

able	apt	bound	due
inclined	liable	likely	prepared
ready	unlikely	unwilling	willing

They were <u>unable to help</u> her.
They were not <u>likely to forget</u> it.

Adjective + 'to' or 'that'

> *I am <u>willing to try</u>.*
> *I'm <u>prepared to say</u> I was wrong.*

4 When you want to express an opinion about someone or something, you often use an adjective followed by a 'to'-infinitive clause.

difficult	easy	impossible	possible	right
wrong				

> *She had been <u>easy to deceive</u>.*
> *The windows will be almost <u>impossible to open</u>.*
> *Am I <u>wrong to stay</u> here?*

Note that in the first two examples, the subject of the main clause is the object of the 'to'-infinitive clause. In the third example, the subject is the same in both clauses.

5 With some adjectives, you use a 'that'-clause to express an opinion about someone or something.

awful	bad	essential	extraordinary
funny	good	important	interesting
obvious	sad	true	

> *I was <u>sad that</u> people had reacted in this way.*
> *It is <u>extraordinary that</u> we should ever have met!*

6 You can also use adjectives with 'to'-infinitive clauses after 'it' as the impersonal subject. You use the preposition 'of' or 'for' to indicate the person or thing that the adjective relates to.

>   *It was <u>easy to find</u> the path.*
>   *It was <u>good of John to help</u> me.*
>   *It was <u>difficult for her to find</u> a job.*

➤ See Unit 17 for 'it' as impersonal subject.

➤ See Unit 47 for more information about adjectives followed by 'of' or 'for'.

'-ing' and '-ed' adjectives

Main points

Many adjectives ending in '-ing' describe the effect that something has on someone's feelings.

Some adjectives ending in '-ing' describe a process or state that continues over a period of time.

Many adjectives ending in '-ed' describe people's feelings.

1 You use many '-ing' adjectives to describe the effect that something has on your feelings, or on the feelings of people in general. For example, if you talk about 'a surprising number', you mean that the number surprises you.

alarming	amazing	annoying
astonishing	boring	charming
confusing	convincing	depressing
disappointing	embarrassing	exciting
frightening	interesting	shocking
surprising	terrifying	tiring
worrying	welcoming	

'-ing' and '-ed' adjectives

He lives in a <u>charming</u> house just outside the town.
She always has a warm <u>welcoming</u> smile.

Most '-ing' adjectives have a related transitive verb.

▶ See Unit 51 for information on transitive verbs.

2 You use some '-ing' adjectives to describe something that continues over a period of time.

ageing	booming	decreasing	dying
existing	increasing	living	remaining

Britain is an <u>ageing</u> society.
<u>Increasing</u> prices are making food very expensive.

These adjectives have related intransitive verbs.

▶ See Unit 51 for information on intransitive verbs.

3 Many '-ed' adjectives describe people's feelings. They have the same form as the past participle of a transitive verb and have a passive meaning. For example, 'a frightened person' is a person who has been frightened by something.

'-ing' and '-ed' adjectives

alarmed	amused	astonished	bored
delighted	depressed	disappointed	excited
frightened	interested	satisfied	shocked
surprised	tired	worried	

> *She looks <u>alarmed</u> about something.*
> *A <u>bored</u> student complained to his teacher.*

Note that the past participles of irregular verbs do not end in '-ed', but can be used as adjectives.
➤ See pages 442–447 for a list of irregular past participles.

> *The bird had a <u>broken</u> wing.*
> *His coat was dirty and <u>torn.</u>*

4 Like other adjectives, '-ing' and '-ed' adjectives can be:

● used in front of a noun

> *They still show <u>amazing</u> loyalty to their parents.*
> *This is the most <u>terrifying</u> tale ever written.*
> *I was thanked by the <u>satisfied</u> customer.*
> *The <u>worried</u> authorities cancelled the match.*

● used after link verbs

> *It's <u>amazing</u> what they can do.*
> *The present situation is <u>terrifying.</u>*
> *He felt <u>satisfied</u> with all the work he had done.*
> *My husband was <u>worried.</u>*

'-ing' and '-ed' adjectives

● modified by adverbials such as 'quite', 'really', and 'very'

> *The film was <u>quite boring.</u>*
> *There is nothing <u>very surprising</u> in this.*
> *She was <u>quite astonished</u> at his behaviour.*
> *He was a <u>very disappointed</u> young man.*

●l used in the comparative and superlative

> *His argument was <u>more convincing</u> than mine.*
> *He became even <u>more depressed</u> after she died.*
> *This is one of <u>the most boring books</u> I've ever read.*
> *She was <u>the most interested</u> in going to the cinema.*

5 A small number of '-ed' adjectives are normally only used after link verbs such as 'be', 'become', or 'feel'. They are related to transitive verbs, and are often followed by a prepositional phrase, a 'to'-infinitive clause, or a 'that'-clause.

convinced	delighted	finished	interested
involved	pleased	prepared	scared
thrilled	tired	touched	

> *The Brazilians are <u>pleased</u> with the results.*
> *He was always <u>prepared</u> to account for his actions.*
> *She was <u>scared</u> that they would find her.*

Comparison: basic forms

Main points

You add '-er' for the comparative and '-est' for the superlative of one-syllable adjectives and adverbs.

You use '-er' and '-est' with some two-syllable adjectives.

You use 'more' for the comparative and 'most' for the superlative of most two-syllable adjectives, all longer adjectives, and adverbs ending in '-ly'.

Some common adjectives and adverbs have irregular forms.

1 You add '-er' for the comparative form and '-est' for the superlative form of one-syllable adjectives and adverbs. If they end in '-e', you add '-r' and '-st'.

cheap	→	cheaper	→	cheapest
safe	→	safer	→	safest

close	cold	fast	hard	large
light	nice	poor	quick	rough
small	weak	wide	young	

Comparison: basic forms

> *They worked <u>harder.</u>*
> *I've found a <u>nicer</u> hotel.*

If they end in a single vowel and consonant (except '-w'), double the consonant.

| big | → | bigger | → | biggest |

| fat | hot | sad | thin | wet |

> *The day grew <u>hotter.</u>*
> *Henry was the <u>biggest</u> of them.*

2. With two-syllable adjectives and adverbs ending in a consonant and '-y', you change the '-y' to '-i' and add '-er' and '-est'.

| happy | → | happier | → | happiest |

| angry | busy | dirty | easy | friendly |
| funny | heavy | lucky | silly | tiny |

> *It couldn't be <u>easier.</u>*
> *That is the <u>funniest</u> bit of the film.*

3. You use 'more' for the comparative and 'most' for the superlative of most two-syllable adjectives, all longer adjectives, and adverbs ending in '-ly'.

Comparison: basic forms

careful	→ more careful	→ most careful
beautiful	→ more beautiful	→ most beautiful
seriously	→ more seriously	→ most seriously

Be <u>more careful</u> next time.

They are the <u>most beautiful</u> gardens in the world.

It affected Clive <u>most seriously.</u>

Note that for 'early' as an adjective or adverb, you use 'earlier' and 'earliest', not 'more' and 'most'.

4 With some common two-syllable adjectives and adverbs you can either add '-er' and '-est', or use 'more' and 'most'.

common	cruel	gentle	handsome
likely	narrow	pleasant	polite
simple	stupid		

Note that 'clever' and 'quiet' only add '-er' and '-est'.

It was <u>quieter</u> outside.

He was the <u>cleverest</u> man I ever knew.

5 You normally use 'the' with superlative adjectives in front of a noun, but you can omit 'the' after a link verb.

It was <u>the happiest</u> day of my life.

I was <u>happiest</u> when I was on my own.

➖ WARNING: When 'most' is used without 'the' in front of adjectives and adverbs, it often means almost the same as 'very'.

This book was <u>most interesting.</u>
I object <u>most strongly.</u>

6 A few common adjectives and adverbs have irregular comparative and superlative forms.

good/well	→	better	→	best
bad/badly	→	worse	→	worst
far	→	farther	→	farthest
		further	→	furthest
old	→	older	→	oldest
		elder	→	eldest

She would ask him when she knew him <u>better.</u>
She sat near the <u>furthest</u> window.

Note that you use 'elder' or 'eldest' to say which brother, sister, or child in a family you mean.

Our <u>eldest</u> daughter couldn't come.

Comparison: uses

Main points

Comparative adjectives are used to compare people or things.

Superlative adjectives are used to say that one person or thing has more of a quality than others in a group or others of that kind.

Comparative adverbs are used in the same way as adjectives.

1 You use comparative adjectives to compare one person or thing with another, or with the same person or thing at another time. After a comparative adjective, you often use 'than'.

> *She was much <u>older than</u> me.*
> *I am <u>happier than</u> I have ever been.*

2 You use a superlative to say that one person or thing has more of a quality than others in a group or others of that kind.

> *Tokyo is Japan's <u>largest city.</u>*
> *He was <u>the tallest person</u> there.*

3 You can use comparative and superlative adjectives in front of a noun.

Comparison: uses

>*I was <u>a better writer</u> than he was.*
>*He had <u>more important things</u> to do.*
>*It was <u>the quickest route</u> from Rome to Naples.*

You can also use comparative and superlative adjectives after link verbs.

>*My brother is <u>younger</u> than me.*
>*He feels <u>more content</u> now.*
>*The sergeant was <u>the tallest.</u>*
>*This book was <u>the most interesting.</u>*

4 You can use adverbs of degree in front of comparative adjectives.

a bit	far	a great deal
good deal	a little	a lot
much	rather	slightly

>*This car's <u>a bit more expensive.</u>*
>*Now I feel <u>a great deal more confident.</u>*
>*It's <u>a rather more complicated</u> story than that.*

You can also use adverbs of degree such as 'by far', 'easily', 'much', or 'quite' in front of 'the' and superlative adjectives.

>*It was <u>by far the worst hospital</u> I had ever seen.*
>*She was <u>easily the most intelligent person</u> in the class.*

Comparison: uses

Note that you can put 'very' between 'the' and a superlative adjective ending in '-est'.

It was of <u>the very highest quality.</u>

5 When you want to say that one situation depends on another, you can use 'the' and a comparative followed by 'the' and another comparative.

<u>The smaller</u> it is, <u>the cheaper</u> it is to post.
<u>The larger</u> the organisation is, <u>the greater</u> the problem of administration becomes.

When you want to say that something increases or decreases, you can use two comparatives linked by 'and'.

It's getting <u>harder and harder</u> to find a job.
Cars are becoming <u>more and more expensive.</u>

6 After a superlative adjective, you can use a prepositional phrase to specify the group you are talking about.

Henry was <u>the biggest of them.</u>
These cakes are probably <u>the best in the world.</u>
He was <u>the most dangerous man in the country.</u>

7 You use the same structures in comparisons using adverbs as those given for adjectives:

Comparison: uses

● 'than' after comparative adverbs

Prices have been rising <u>faster than</u> incomes.

● 'the' and a comparative adverb followed by 'the' and another comparative adverb

<u>The quicker</u> we finish, <u>the sooner</u> we will go home.

● two comparative adverbs linked by 'and'

He sounded <u>worse and worse.</u>
He drove <u>faster and faster</u> till we told him to stop.

Main points

This includes words like: 'as…as', 'the same (as)' and 'like'.

You use 'as…as…' to compare people or things.

You can also compare people or things by using 'the same (as)'.

You can also compare people or things by using a link verb and a phrase beginning with 'like'.

1 You use 'as…as…' to compare people or things that are similar in some way.

You use 'as' and an adjective or adverb, followed by 'as' and a noun group, an adverbial, or a clause.

> You're <u>as bad as your sister.</u>
> The airport was <u>as crowded as ever.</u>
> I am <u>as good as she is.</u>
> Let us examine it <u>as carefully as we can.</u>

2 You can make a negative comparison using 'not as…as…' or 'not so…as…'.

> The food <u>wasn't as</u> good <u>as</u> yesterday.

Other ways of comparing

They are <u>not as</u> clever <u>as</u> they appear to be.
He is <u>not so</u> old <u>as</u> I thought.

3. You can use the adverbs 'almost', 'just', 'nearly', or 'quite' in front of 'as…as…'.

He was <u>almost as</u> fast <u>as</u> his brother.
Mary was <u>just as</u> pale <u>as</u> before.
She was <u>nearly as</u> tall <u>as</u> he was.

In a negative comparison, you can use 'not nearly' or 'not quite' before 'as…as…'.

This is <u>not nearly as</u> complicated <u>as</u> it sounds.
The hotel was <u>not quite as</u> good <u>as</u> they expected.

4. When you want to say that one thing is very similar to something else, you can use 'the same as' followed by a noun group, an adverbial, or a clause.

Your bag is <u>the same as</u> mine.
I said <u>the same as</u> always.
She looked <u>the same as</u> she did yesterday.

If people or things are very similar or identical, you can also say that they are 'the same'.

Teenage fashions are <u>the same</u> all over the world.
The initial stage of learning English is <u>the same</u> for many students.

You can use some adverbs in front of 'the same as' or 'the same'.

almost	exactly	just	more or less
much	nearly	roughly	virtually

He did <u>exactly the same as</u> John did.
You two look <u>almost the same.</u>

You can use 'the same' in front of a noun group, with or without 'as' after the noun group.

They reached almost <u>the same height.</u>
It was painted <u>the same colour as</u> the wall.

5 You can also compare people or things by using a link verb such as 'be', 'feel', 'look', or 'seem' and a phrase beginning with 'like'.

It <u>was like</u> a dream.
He still <u>feels like</u> a child.
He <u>looked like</u> an actor.
The houses <u>seemed like</u> mansions.

You can use some adverbs in front of 'like'.

a bit	a little	exactly	just
least	less	more	most
quite	rather	somewhat	very

He looks <u>just like</u> a baby.
Of all his children, she was the one <u>most like</u> me.

Other ways of comparing

6 If the noun group after 'as' or 'like' in any of these structures is a pronoun, you use an object pronoun or possessive pronoun.

> *Jane was as clever as <u>him.</u>*
> *His car is the same as <u>mine.</u>*

7 You can also use 'less' and 'least' to make comparisons with the opposite meaning to 'more' and 'most'.

> *They were <u>less fortunate</u> than us.*
> *He was <u>the least skilled</u> of the workers.*
> *We see him <u>less frequently</u> than we used to.*

Adverbials

Main points

Adverbials are usually adverbs, adverb phrases, or prepositional phrases.

Adverbials of manner, place, and time are used to say how, where, or when something happens.

Adverbials usually come after the verb, or after the object if there is one.

The usual order of adverbials is manner, then place, then time.

---

1 An adverbial is often one word, an adverb.

> *Sit there <u>quietly</u>, and listen to this music.*
> *Come here <u>immediately</u>!*

However, an adverbial can also be a group of words:

● an adverb phrase

> *He did not play <u>well enough</u> to win.*

● a prepositional phrase

> *The children were playing <u>in the park</u>.*

Adverbials

● a noun group, usually a time expression

Come and see me <u>next week.</u>

2 You use an adverbial of manner to describe the way in which something happens or is done.

They looked <u>anxiously</u> at each other.
She listened <u>with great patience</u> as he told his story.

You use an adverbial of place to say where something happens.

A plane flew <u>overhead.</u>
No birds or animals came <u>near the body.</u>

You use an adverbial of time to say when something happens.

She will be here <u>soon.</u>
He was born <u>on 3 April 1925.</u>

3 You normally put adverbials of manner, place, and time after the main verb.

She sang <u>beautifully.</u>
The book was lying <u>on the table.</u>
The car broke down <u>yesterday.</u>

If the verb has an object, you put the adverbial after the object.

I did learn to play a few tunes <u>very badly.</u>
Thomas made his decision <u>immediately.</u>
He took the glasses <u>to the kitchen.</u>

If you are using more than one of these adverbials in a clause, the usual order is manner, then place, then time.

They were sitting <u>quite happily in the car.</u>
(manner, place)
She spoke <u>very well at the village hall last night.</u>
(manner, place, time)

4 You usually put adverbials of frequency, probability, and duration in front of the main verb.

She <u>occasionally comes</u> to my house.
You have <u>very probably heard</u> the news by now.
They had <u>already given</u> me the money.

A few adverbs of degree also usually come in front of the main verb.

She <u>really enjoyed</u> the party.

5 When you want to focus on an adverbial, you can do this by putting it in a different place in the clause:

● you can put an adverbial at the beginning of a clause, usually for emphasis

Adverbials

Slowly, he opened his eyes.
In September I travelled to California.
Next to the coffee machine stood a pile of cups.

Note that after adverbials of place, as in the last example, the verb can come in front of the subject.

● you can sometimes put adverbs and adverb phrases in front of the main verb for emphasis, but not prepositional phrases or noun groups

He deliberately chose it because it was cheap.
I very much wanted to go with them.

● you can change the order of adverbials of manner, place, and time when you want to change the emphasis

They were sitting in the car quite happily.
(place, manner)
At the meeting last night, she spoke very well.
(place, time, manner)

Adverbials of manner

Main points

Most adverbs of manner are formed by adding '-ly' to an adjective, but sometimes other spelling changes are needed.

You cannot form adverbs from adjectives that end in '-ly'.

Some adverbs have the same form as adjectives.

You do not use adverbs after link verbs, you use adjectives.

Adverbials of manner are sometimes prepositional phrases or noun groups.

1. Adverbs of manner are often formed by adding '-ly' to an adjective.

Adjectives:	bad	beautiful	careful	quick
	quiet	soft		
Adverbs:	badly	beautifully	carefully	
	quickly	quietly	softly	

2. Adverbs formed in this way usually have a similar meaning to the adjective.

She is as clever as she is <u>beautiful.</u>

Adverbials of manner

He talked so politely and danced so <u>beautifully</u>.
'We must not talk. We must be <u>quiet</u>,' said Sita.
She wanted to sit <u>quietly</u>, to relax.

3 There are sometimes changes in spelling when an adverb is formed from an adjective.

'-le' changes to '-ly':	gentle → gently
'-y' changes to '-ily':	easy → easily
'-ic' changes to '-ically':	automatic → automatically
'-ue' changes to '-uly':	true → truly
'-ll' changes to '-lly':	full → fully

Note that 'public' changes to 'publicly', not 'publically'.

● WARNING: You cannot form adverbs from adjectives that already end in '-ly'. For example, you cannot say 'He smiled at me friendlily'. You can sometimes use a prepositional phrase instead: 'He smiled at me in a friendly way'.

4 Some adverbs of manner have the same form as adjectives and have similar meanings, for example 'fast', 'hard', and 'late'.

I've always been interested in <u>fast</u> cars.
(adjective)
The driver was driving too <u>fast</u>. (adverb)

Adverbials of manner

Note that 'hardly' and 'lately' are not adverbs of manner and have different meanings from the adjectives 'hard' and 'late'.

> *It was a <u>hard</u> decision to make.*
> *I <u>hardly</u> had any time to talk to her.*
> *The train was <u>late</u> as usual.*
> *Have you seen John <u>lately</u>?*

5 The adverb of manner related to the adjective 'good' is 'well'.

> *He is a <u>good</u> dancer.*
> *He dances <u>well</u>.*

Note that 'well' can sometimes be an adjective when it refers to someone's health.

> *'How are you?' – 'I am very <u>well</u>, thank you.'*

6 You do not use adverbs after link verbs such as 'be', 'become', 'feel', 'get', 'look', and 'seem'. You use an adjective after these verbs. For example, you do not say 'Sue felt happily'. You say 'Sue felt happy'.

▶ See Unit 73 for more information on link verbs.

7 You do not often use prepositional phrases or noun groups as adverbials of manner. However, you occasionally need to use them, for example when

Adverbials of manner

there is no adverb form available. The prepositional phrases and noun groups usually include a noun such as 'way', 'fashion', or 'manner', or a noun that refers to someone's voice.

> She asked me <u>in such a nice manner</u> that I couldn't refuse.
> He did it <u>the right way.</u>
> They spoke <u>in angry tones.</u>

Prepositional phrases with 'like' are also used as adverbials of manner.

> I slept <u>like a baby.</u>
> He drove <u>like a madman.</u>

Adverbials of time

Main points

Adverbials of time can be time expressions such as 'last night'.

Adverbials of time can be prepositional phrases with 'at', 'in', or 'on'.

'For' refers to a period of time in the past, present, or future.

'Since' refers to a point in past time.

1 You use adverbials of time to say when something happens. You often use noun groups called time expressions as adverbials of time.

yesterday	today
tomorrow	last night
last year	next Saturday
next week	the day after tomorrow
the other day	

Note that you do not use the prepositions 'at', 'in', or 'on' with time expressions.

One of my children wrote to me <u>today</u>.
So, you're coming back <u>next week?</u>

You often use time expressions with verbs in the

Adverbials of time

present tense to talk about the future.

> *The plane leaves <u>tomorrow morning.</u>*
> *They're coming <u>next week.</u>*

2 You can use prepositional phrases as adverbials of time:

● 'at' is used with:

clock times:	at eight o'clock, at three fifteen
religious festivals:	at Christmas, at Easter
mealtimes:	at breakfast, at lunchtimes
specific periods:	at night, at the weekend, at weekends, at half-term

● 'in' is used with:

seasons:	in autumn, in the spring
years and centuries:	in 1985, in the year 2000, in the nineteenth century
months:	in July, in December
parts of the day:	in the morning, in the evenings

Note that you also use 'in' to say that something will happen during or after a period of time in the future.

> *I think we'll find out <u>in</u> the next few days.*

Adverbials of time

● 'on' is used with:

days:	on Monday, on Tuesday morning, on Sunday evenings
special days:	on Christmas Day, on my birthday, on his wedding anniversary
dates:	on the twentieth of July, on June 21st

3 You use 'for' with verbs in any tense to say how long something continues to happen.

> He *is* in Italy *for* a month.
> I *remained* silent *for* a long time.

⊖ WARNING: You do not use 'during' to say how long something continues to happen. You cannot say 'I went there during three weeks'.

4 You use 'since' with a verb in the present perfect or past perfect tense to say when something started to happen.

> Marilyn *has lived* in Paris *since* 1984.
> I *had eaten* nothing *since* breakfast.

5 You can use many other prepositional phrases as adverbials of time. You use:
● 'during' and 'over' for a period of time in which something happens

> I saw him twice *during* the holidays.
> Will you stay here *over* Christmas?

Adverbials of time

● 'from…to/till/until' and 'between…and' for the beginning and end of a period of time

> *The building is closed <u>from</u> April <u>to</u> May.*
> *She worked <u>from</u> four o'clock <u>till</u> ten o'clock.*
> *Can you take the test <u>between</u> now <u>and</u> June?*

● 'by' when you mean 'not later than'

> <u>*By*</u> *eleven o'clock, Brody was back in his office.*
> *Can we get this finished <u>by</u> tomorrow?*

● 'before' and 'after'

> *I saw him <u>before</u> the match.*
> *She left the house <u>after</u> ten o'clock.*

'Since', 'till', 'until', 'after', and 'before' can also be conjunctions with time clauses.

➤ See Unit 96.

> *I've been wearing glasses <u>since I was three.</u>*

6 You use the adverb 'ago' with the past simple to say how long before the time of speaking something happened. You always put 'ago' after the period of time.

> *We saw him about a month <u>ago.</u>*
> *John's wife died five years <u>ago.</u>*

⊖ WARNING: You do not use 'ago' with the present perfect tense. You cannot say 'We have gone to Spain two years ago'.

Frequency and probability

Main points

This includes words like: 'always', 'ever', 'never', 'perhaps', 'possibly' and 'probably'.

Adverbials of frequency are used to say how often something happens.

Adverbials of probability are used to say how sure you are about something.

These adverbials usually come before the main verb, but they come after 'be' as a main verb.

1 You use adverbials of frequency to say how often something happens.

a lot	always	ever	frequently
hardly ever	never	normally	occasionally
often	rarely	sometimes	usually

We <u>often</u> swam in the sea.
She <u>never</u> comes to my parties.
You must have noticed how tired he <u>sometimes</u> looks.

Frequency and probability

2 You use adverbials of probability to say how sure you are about something.

certainly	definitely	maybe	obviously
perhaps	possibly	probably	really

> I _definitely_ saw her yesterday.
> The driver _probably_ knows the quickest and
> best route.
> _Maybe_ he sincerely wanted to help his country.

3 You usually put adverbials of frequency and probability before the main verb and after an auxiliary or a modal.

> He _sometimes works_ downstairs in the
> restaurant kitchen.
> You _are definitely wasting_ your time.
> I _have never had_ such a horrible meal!
> I _shall never forget_ this day.

Note that you usually put them after 'be' as a main verb.

> He _is always_ careful with his money.
> You _are probably_ right.
> Today's inflation figure is _certainly_ much too
> high.

'Perhaps' usually comes at the beginning of the sentence.

> *Perhaps the beaches are cleaner in the north.*
> *Perhaps you need a current membership card to get in.*

'A lot' always comes after the main verb.

> *I go swimming a lot in the summer.*

4 'Never' is a negative adverb.

> *She never goes abroad.*
> *I've never been to Europe.*

You normally use 'ever' in questions, negative sentences, and 'if'-clauses.

> *Have you ever been to a football match?*
> *Don't ever do that again!*
> *If you ever need anything, just call me.*

Note that you can sometimes use 'ever' in affirmative sentences, for example after a superlative.

> *She is the best dancer I have ever seen.*
> *This is the most awful evening I can ever remember.*

Frequency and probability

You use 'hardly ever' in affirmative sentences to mean almost never.

> *We <u>hardly ever</u> meet.*
> *We ate chips every night, but <u>hardly ever</u> had fish.*

Adverbials of duration

Main points

'Already' is used to say that something has happened earlier than expected.

'Still' is used to say that something continues to happen until a particular time.

'Yet' is used to say that something has not happened before a particular time.

'Any longer', 'any more', 'no longer', and 'no more' are used to say that something has stopped happening.

1 You use adverbials of duration to say that an event or situation is continuing, stopping, or is not happening at the moment.

> *She <u>still</u> lives in London.*
> *I couldn't stand it <u>any more.</u>*
> *It isn't dark <u>yet.</u>*

2 You use 'already' to say that something has happened sooner than it was expected to happen. You put 'already' in front of the main verb.

> *He had <u>already bought</u> the cups and saucers.*

Adverbials of duration

I've <u>already seen</u> them.
The guests were <u>already coming</u> in.

You put 'already' after 'be' as a main verb.

Julie was <u>already</u> in bed.

You can also use 'already' to emphasize that something is the case, for example when someone else does not know or is not sure.

I am <u>already</u> aware of that problem.

You do not normally use 'already' in negative statements, but you can use it in negative 'if'-clauses.

Show it to him <u>if he hasn't already seen it.</u>

You can put 'already' at the beginning or end of a clause for emphasis.

<u>Already</u> he was calculating the profit he could make.
I've done it <u>already.</u>

3 You use 'still' to say that a situation continues to exist up to a particular time in the past, present, or future. You put 'still' in front of the main verb.

We <u>were still waiting</u> for the election results.
My family <u>still live</u> in India.
You <u>will still get</u> tickets, if you hurry.

Adverbials of duration

You put 'still' after 'be' as a main verb.

> *Martin's mother died, but his father <u>is still</u> alive.*

You can use 'still' after the subject and before the verb group in negative sentences to express surprise or impatience.

> *You <u>still</u> haven't given us the keys.*
> *He <u>still</u> didn't say a word.*
> *It was after midnight, and he <u>still</u> wouldn't leave.*

Remember that you can use 'still' at the beginning of a clause with a similar meaning to 'after all' or 'nevertheless'.

> <u>*Still,*</u> *he is my brother, so I'll have to help him.*
> <u>*Still,*</u> *it's not too bad. We didn't lose all the money.*

4 You use 'yet' at the end of negative sentences and questions to say that something has not happened or had not happened up to a particular time, but is or was expected to happen later.

> *We haven't got the tickets <u>yet.</u>*
> *Have you joined the swimming club <u>yet?</u>*
> *They hadn't seen the baby <u>yet.</u>*

Remember that 'yet' can also be used at the beginning of a clause with a similar meaning to 'but'.

Adverbials of duration

> *I don't miss her, <u>yet</u> I do often wonder where she went.*
>
> *They know they won't win. <u>Yet</u> they keep on trying.*

5 You use 'any longer' and 'any more' at the end of negative clauses to say that a past situation has ended and does not exist now or will not exist in the future.

> *I wanted the job, but I couldn't wait <u>any longer.</u>*
> *He's not going to play <u>any more.</u>*

In formal English, you can use an affirmative clause with 'no longer' and 'no more'. You can put them at the end of the clause, or in front of the main verb.

> *He could stand the pain <u>no more.</u>*
> *He <u>no longer</u> wanted to buy it.*

Adverbials of degree

Main points

Adverbs of degree usually modify verbs.

Some adverbs of degree can modify adjectives, other adverbs, or clauses.

1. You use adverbs of degree to modify verbs. They make the verb stronger or weaker.

   I <u>totally disagree.</u>
   I can <u>nearly swim.</u>

2. Some adverbs can come in front of a main verb, after a main verb, or after the object if there is one.

badly	completely	greatly	seriously
strongly	totally		

   Mr Brooke <u>strongly</u> criticized them.
   I disagree <u>completely</u> with John Taylor.
   That argument doesn't convince me <u>totally.</u>

   Some adverbs are mostly used in front of the verb.

almost	largely	nearly	really	quite

   He <u>almost</u> crashed into a lorry.

Adverbials of degree

Note that 'really' is used at the beginning of a clause to express surprise, and at the end of a clause as an adverb of manner.

> _Really,_ I didn't know that!
> He wanted it _really,_ but was too shy to ask.

'A lot' and 'very much' come after the main verb if there is no object, or after the object.

> She helped _a lot._
> We liked him _very much._

'Very much' can come after the subject and in front of verbs like 'want', 'prefer', and 'enjoy'.

> I _very much_ wanted to take it with me.

3 | Some adverbs of degree go in front of adjectives or other adverbs and modify them.

awfully	extremely	fairly	pretty	quite
rather	really	very		

> …a _fairly large_ office, with filing space.

Note that you can use 'rather' before or after 'a' or 'an' followed by an adjective and a noun.

> Seaford is _rather a_ pleasant town.
> It is _a rather_ complicated story.

When 'quite' means 'fairly', you put it in front of 'a' or 'an' followed by an adjective and a noun.

Adverbials of degree

My father gave me <u>quite a large sum</u> of money.

However, when 'quite' means 'extremely', you can put it after 'a'. You can say 'a quite enormous sum'.

4 You use some adverbs of degree to modify clauses and prepositional phrases.

| entirely | just | largely | mainly | partly | simply |

Are you saying that <u>simply because I am here?</u>
I don't think it's worth going <u>just for a day.</u>

5 You use 'so' and 'such' to emphasize a quality that someone or something has. 'So' can be followed by an adjective, an adverb, or a noun group beginning with 'many', 'much', 'few', or 'little'.

John is <u>so interesting</u> to talk to.
Science is changing <u>so rapidly.</u>
I want to do <u>so many</u> different things.

'Such' is followed by a singular noun group with 'a', or a plural noun group.

There was <u>such a noise</u> we couldn't hear.
They said <u>such nasty things.</u>

⊖ WARNING: 'So' is never followed by a singular noun group with 'a' or a plural noun group.

Adverbials of degree

6 You use 'too' when you mean 'more than is necessary' or 'more than is good'. You can use 'too' before adjectives and adverbs, and before 'many', 'much', 'few', or 'little'.

> *The prices are <u>too high.</u>*
> *I've been paying <u>too much</u> tax.*

You use 'enough' after adjectives and adverbs.

> *I waited until my daughter was <u>old enough</u> to read.*
> *He didn't work <u>quickly enough.</u>*

Note that 'enough' is also a determiner.

> *We've got <u>enough money</u> to buy that car now.*

7 You use emphasizing adverbs to modify adjectives such as 'astonishing', 'furious', and 'wonderful', which express extreme qualities.

absolutely	completely	entirely	perfectly
purely	quite	really	simply
totally	utterly		

> *I think he's <u>absolutely wonderful.</u>*

Place and direction

Main points

This includes words like: 'above', 'below', 'down', 'from', 'to', 'towards' and 'up'.

You normally use prepositional phrases to say where a person or thing is, or the direction they are moving in.

You can also use adverbs and adverb phrases for place and direction.

Many words are both prepositions and adverbs.

1 You use prepositions to talk about the place where someone or something is. Prepositions are always followed by a noun group, which is called the object of the preposition.

above	among	at	behind
below	beneath	beside	between
in	inside	near	on
opposite	outside	over	round
through	under	underneath	

He stood <u>near</u> the door.

Place and direction

Two minutes later we were safely <u>inside</u> the taxi.
Two young people sat <u>opposite</u> me.

Note that some prepositions consist of more than one word.

| in between | in front of | next to | on top of |

There was a man standing <u>in front of</u> me.
She sat down <u>next to</u> him on the sofa.
The books were piled <u>on top of</u> each other.

2 You can also use prepositions to talk about the direction that someone or something is moving in, or the place that someone or something is moving towards.

across	along	back to	down	into
onto	out of	past	round	through
to	towards	up		

He watched Karl run <u>across</u> the street.
They dived <u>into</u> the water.
She turned and rushed <u>out of</u> the room.

3 Many prepositions can be used both for place and direction.

The bank is just <u>across</u> the High Street. (place)
I walked <u>across</u> the room. (direction)

Place and direction

We live in the big old house <u>over</u> the road.
(place)
I stole his keys and escaped <u>over</u> the wall.
(direction)

4 You can also use adverbs and adverb phrases for place and direction.

abroad	away	downstairs
downwards	here	indoors
outdoors	there	underground
upstairs	anywhere	everywhere
nowhere	somewhere	

Sheila was <u>here</u> a moment ago.
Can't you go <u>upstairs</u> and turn the bedroom light off?

Note that a few noun groups can also be used as adverbials of place or direction.

Steve lives <u>next door</u> at number 23.
I thought we went <u>the other way</u> last time we came.

5 Many words can be used as prepositions and as adverbs, with no difference in meaning. Remember

Place and direction

that prepositions have noun groups as objects, but adverbs do not.

> *Did he fall <u>down the stairs?</u>*
> *Please do sit <u>down.</u>*
> *I looked <u>underneath the bed,</u> but the box had gone!*
> *Always put a sheet of paper <u>underneath.</u>*

Place – 'at', 'in', 'on'

Main points

You use 'at' to talk about a place as a point.

You use 'in' to talk about a place as an area.

You use 'on' to talk about a place as a surface.

1 You use 'at' when you are thinking of a place as a point in space.

> *She waited <u>at the bus stop</u> for over twenty minutes.*
> *'Where were you last night?' – '<u>At Mick's house.</u>'*

2 You also use 'at' with words such as 'back', 'bottom', 'end', 'front', and 'top' to talk about the different parts of a place.

> *Mrs Castle was waiting <u>at the bottom</u> of the stairs.*
> *They escaped by a window <u>at the back</u> of the house.*
> *I saw a taxi <u>at the end</u> of the street.*

You use 'at' with public places and institutions. Note that you also say 'at home' and 'at work'.

> *I have to be <u>at the station</u> by ten o'clock.*

Place – 'at', 'in', 'on'

We landed <u>at a small airport.</u>
A friend of mine is <u>at Training College.</u>
She wanted to stay <u>at home.</u>

You say 'at the corner' or 'on the corner' when you are talking about streets.

The car was parked <u>at the corner</u> of the street.
There's a telephone box <u>on the corner.</u>

You say 'in the corner' when you are talking about a room.

She put the chair <u>in the corner</u> of the room.

3. You use 'in' when you are talking about a place as an area. You use 'in' with:

- a country or geographical region

When I was <u>in Spain,</u> it was terribly cold.
A thousand homes <u>in the east of Scotland</u> suffered power cuts.

- a city, town, or village

I've been teaching at a college <u>in London.</u>

- a building when you are talking about people or things inside it

They were sitting having dinner <u>in the restaurant.</u>

187

You also use 'in' with containers of any kind when talking about things inside them.

> *She kept the cards <u>in a little box.</u>*

4 Compare the use of 'at' and 'in' in these examples.

> *I had a hard day <u>at the office.</u>* ('at' emphasizes the office as a public place or institution)
> *I left my coat behind <u>in the office.</u>*
> ('in' emphasizes the office as a building)
> *There's a good film <u>at the cinema.</u>*
> ('at' emphasizes the cinema as a public place)
> *It was very cold <u>in the cinema.</u>* ('in' emphasizes the cinema as a building.)

5 When talking about addresses, you use 'at' when you give the house number, and 'in' when you just give the name of the street.

> *They used to live <u>at 5, Weston Road.</u>*
> *She got a job <u>in Oxford Street.</u>*

Note that American English uses 'on': 'He lived on Penn Street.'

You use 'at' when you are talking about someone's house.

> *I'll see you <u>at Fred's house.</u>*

Place – 'at', 'in', 'on'

6 You use 'on' when you are talking about a place as a surface. You can also use 'on top of'.

> *I sat down <u>on the sofa.</u>*
> *She put her keys <u>on top of the television.</u>*

You also use 'on' when you are thinking of a place as a point on a line, such as a road, a railway line, a river, or a coastline.

> *Scrabster is <u>on the north coast.</u>*
> *Oxford is <u>on the A34</u> between Birmingham and London.*

▶ See Unit 40 for information on 'at', 'in', and 'on' in adverbials of time.

Transport prepositions

Main points

This includes phrases like: 'by bus', 'in a car', 'on the plane', and 'off the train'.

You can use 'by' with most forms of transport.

You use 'in', 'into', and 'out of' with cars.

You normally use 'on', 'onto', and 'off' with other forms of transport.

1 When you talk about the type of vehicle or transport you use to travel somewhere, you use 'by'.

> by bus   by bicycle   by car   by coach   by plane
> by train

> *She had come <u>by car</u> with her husband.*
> *I went <u>by bus and train</u> to Nottingham.*

⊖ WARNING: If you want to say you walk somewhere, you say you go 'on foot', not 'by foot'.

> *Marie decided to continue <u>on foot.</u>*

2 You use 'in', 'into', and 'out of' when you are talking about cars, vans, lorries, taxis, and ambulances.

> *I followed them <u>in my car.</u>*

190

Transport prepositions

The carpets had to be collected <u>in a van.</u>
Mr Ward happened to be getting <u>into his lorry.</u>
She was carried <u>out of the ambulance</u> and up the steps.

3 You use 'on', 'onto', and 'off' when you are talking about other forms of transport, such as buses, coaches, trains, ships, and planes.

Why don't you come <u>on the train</u> with me to New York?
He was already <u>on the plane</u> from California.
The last thing he wanted was to spend ten days <u>on a boat</u> with Hooper.
He jumped back <u>onto the old bus.</u>
Mr Bixby stepped <u>off the train</u> and walked quickly to the exit.

You can use 'in', 'into', and 'out of' with these other forms of transport, usually when you are focusing on the physical position or movement of the person, rather than stating what form of transport they are using.

The passengers <u>in the plane</u> were beginning to panic.
He got back <u>into the train</u> quickly, before Batt could stop him.
We jumped <u>out of the bus</u> and ran into the nearest shop.

Adjective + preposition

Main points

Some adjectives used after link verbs can be used alone or followed by a prepositional phrase.

Some adjectives must be followed by particular prepositions.

Some adjectives can be followed by different prepositions to introduce different types of information.

1 When you use an adjective after a link verb, you can often use the adjective on its own or followed by a prepositional phrase.
➤ See Unit 33.

He was <u>afraid.</u>
He was <u>afraid of</u> his enemies.

2 Some adjectives cannot be used alone after a link verb. If they are followed by a prepositional phrase, it must have a particular preposition:

| aware of | accustomed to | unaware of |
| unaccustomed to | fond of | used to |

I've always been terribly <u>fond of</u> you.
He is <u>unaccustomed to</u> the heat.

Adjective + preposition

3 Some adjectives can be used alone, or followed by a particular preposition:

● used alone, or with 'of' to specify the cause of a feeling

afraid	ashamed	convinced	critical
envious	frightened	jealous	proud
scared	suspicious	terrified	tired

They may feel <u>jealous of</u> your success.
I was <u>terrified of</u> her.

● used alone, or with 'of' to specify the person who has a quality

brave	careless	clever	generous	good
intelligent	kind	nice	polite	sensible
silly	stupid	thoughtful	unkind	
unreasonable	wrong			

That was <u>clever of</u> you!
I turned the job down, which was <u>stupid of</u> me.

● used alone or used with 'to', usually referring to:

similarity:	close equal identical related similar
marriage:	married engaged
loyalty:	dedicated devoted loyal
rank:	junior senior

Adjective + preposition

My problems are very <u>similar to</u> yours.
He was <u>dedicated to</u> his job.

● used alone, or followed by 'with' to specify the cause of a feeling

bored	content	displeased
dissatisfied	impatient	impressed
pleased	satisfied	

I could never be <u>bored with</u> football.
He was <u>pleased with</u> her.

● used alone, or with 'at', usually referring to:

strong reactions:	alarmed amazed
	astonished shocked
	surprised
ability:	bad excellent good
	hopeless useless

He was <u>shocked at</u> the hatred they had known.
She had always been <u>good at</u> languages.

● used alone, or with 'for' to specify the person or thing that a quality relates to

common	difficult	easy	essential
important	necessary	possible	unnecessary
unusual	usual		

Adjective + preposition

It's <u>difficult for young people</u> on their own.
It was <u>unusual for them</u> to go away at the weekend.

4 Some adjectives can be used alone, or used with different prepositions.

● used alone, with an impersonal subject and 'of' and the subject of the action, or with a personal subject and 'to' and the object of the action

cruel	friendly	generous	good
kind	mean	nasty	nice
polite	rude	unfriendly	unkind

It was <u>rude of</u> him to leave so suddenly.
She was <u>rude to</u> him for no reason.

● used alone, with 'about' to specify a thing or 'with' to specify a person

angry	annoyed	delighted	disappointed
fed up	furious	happy	upset

She was still <u>angry about</u> the result.
They're getting pretty <u>fed up with</u> him.

Noun + preposition

Main points

'Of' can be used to add many different types of information, 'with' is used to specify a quality or possession.

Some nouns are always followed by particular prepositions.

---

1. You can give more information about a noun by adding a prepositional phrase after it.

    Four men <u>on holiday</u> were in the car.
    A sound <u>behind him</u> made him turn.

2. You often use the preposition 'of' after a noun to add various kinds of information. For example, you can use 'of' to indicate:

    ● what something is made of or consists of

    ...a wall <u>of stone.</u>
    A feeling <u>of panic</u> was rising in him.

    ● what the subject matter of speech, writing, or a picture is

    She gave a brief account <u>of her interview.</u>
    There was a picture <u>of them both</u> in the paper.

Noun + preposition

● what a person or thing belongs to or is connected with

> *She was the daughter <u>of the village priest.</u>*
> *The boys sat on the floor <u>of the living room.</u>*

● what qualities a person or thing has

> *She was a woman <u>of energy and ambition.</u>*
> *They faced problems <u>of great complexity.</u>*

3 After nouns referring to actions, you use 'of' to indicate the subject or object of the action.

> *…the arrival <u>of the police.</u>*
> *…the destruction <u>of their city.</u>*

After nouns referring to people who perform an action, you use 'of' to say what the action involves or is aimed at.

> *…supporters <u>of the hunger strike.</u>*
> *…a student <u>of English.</u>*

Note that you often use two nouns, rather than a noun and a prepositional phrase. For example, you say 'bank robbers', not 'robbers of the bank'.

4 After nouns referring to measurement, you use 'of' to give the exact figure.

> *…an average temperature <u>of 20 degrees.</u>*
> *…a speed <u>of 25 kilometres an hour.</u>*

Noun + preposition

You can use 'of' after a noun to give someone's age.

Jonathan was a child <u>of seven</u> when it happened.

5 You use 'with' after a noun to say that a person or thing has a particular quality, feature, or possession.

…a girl <u>with red hair</u>.
…the man <u>with the gun</u>.

Note that you use 'in' after a noun to say what someone is wearing.

…a grey-haired man <u>in a raincoat</u>.
…the man <u>in dark glasses</u>.

6 Some nouns are usually followed by a particular preposition. Here are some examples of:

● nouns followed by 'to'

alternative	answer	approach	attitude
introduction	invitation	reaction	reference
resistance	return		

This was my first real <u>introduction to</u> Africa.

● nouns followed by 'for'

admiration	desire	dislike	need
reason	respect	responsibility	search
substitute	taste	thirst	

Their <u>need for</u> money is growing fast.

Noun + preposition

● nouns followed by 'on'

| agreement | attack | comment | effect | tax |

She had a dreadful <u>effect on</u> me.

● nouns followed by 'with' or 'between'

| connection | contact | link | relationship |

His illness had some <u>connection with</u> his diet.

● nouns followed by 'in'

| decrease | difficulty | fall | increase | rise |

They demanded a large <u>increase in</u> wages.

Verb + preposition

Main points

Some verbs do not take an object and are normally followed by a preposition.

Some verbs take an object followed by a particular preposition.

Some verbs can take either an object or a preposition.

1. Many verbs that are used without an object are normally followed by a prepositional phrase. Some verbs take a particular preposition:

belong to	consist of	hint at
hope for	insist on	lead to
listen to	pay for	qualify for
refer to	relate to	sympathize with

The land <u>belongs to</u> a rich family.
She then <u>referred to</u> the Minister's report.

2. With other verbs that are used without an object, the choice of a different preposition may alter the meaning of the clause.

Verbs + preposition

agree on/with	appeal for/to
apologize for/to	conform to/with
result from/in	suffer from/with

They <u>agreed on</u> a plan of action.
You <u>agreed with</u> me that we should buy a car.
His failure <u>resulted from</u> lack of attention to details.
The match <u>resulted in</u> a draw.

3 With verbs that are used without an object, different prepositions are used to introduce different types of information.

● 'about' indicates the subject matter

care	complain	dream	explain	hear
know	speak	talk	think	write

We will always <u>care about</u> freedom.
Tonight I'm going to <u>talk about</u> engines.

● 'at' indicates direction

glance	glare	grin	laugh	look	shout
smile	stare				

I don't know why he was <u>laughing at</u> that joke.
'Hey!' she <u>shouted at</u> him.

Verb + preposition

● 'for' indicates purpose or reason

apologize	apply	ask	look	wait

> *He wanted to <u>apologize for</u> being late.*
> *I'm going to <u>wait for</u> the next bus.*

● 'into' indicates the object involved in a collision

bump	crash	drive	run

> *His car <u>crashed into</u> the wall.*
> *She <u>drove into</u> the back of a lorry.*

● 'of' indicates facts or information

hear	know	speak	talk	think

> *I've <u>heard of</u> him but I don't know who he is.*
> *Do you <u>know of</u> the new plans for the sports centre?*

● 'on' indicates confidence or certainty

count	depend	plan	rely

> *You can <u>count on</u> me.*
> *You can <u>rely on</u> him to be polite.*

Verb + preposition

● 'to' indicates the listener or reader

| complain | explain | listen | say | speak |
| talk | write | | | |

> *They <u>complained to</u> me about the noise.*
> *Mary turned her head to <u>speak to</u> him.*

● 'with' indicates someone whose opinion is the same or different

| agree | argue | disagree | side |

> *Do you <u>agree with</u> me about this?*
> *The daughters <u>sided with</u> their mothers.*

4 Some verbs have an object, but are also followed by a preposition.

> *The police <u>accused</u> him <u>of</u> murder.*
> *They <u>borrowed</u> some money <u>from</u> the bank.*

Some verbs can take either an object or a prepositional phrase with no change in meaning.

> *He had to fight <u>them</u>.*
> *He was fighting <u>against history.</u>*

Phrasal verbs

Main points

A phrasal verb is a combination of a verb and an adverb or preposition.

The usual meaning of the verb is normally altered.

Phrasal verbs are used in four main structures.

---

1. Phrasal verbs are verbs that combine with adverbs or prepositions. The adverbs and prepositions are called particles, for example 'down', 'in', 'off', 'out', and 'up'.

> She _turned off_ the radio.
> Mr Knight offered to _put_ him _up._

2. Phrasal verbs extend the usual meaning of the verb or create a new meaning. For example, if you 'break' something, you damage it, but if you 'break out of' a place, you escape from it.

> They _broke out of_ prison on Thursday night.
> The pain gradually _wore off._

3. Phrasal verbs are normally used in one of four main structures. In the first structure, the verb is followed by a particle, and there is no object.

Phrasal verbs

break out	catch on	check up	come in
get by	give in	go away	grow up
look in	ring off	start out	stay up
stop off	wait up	watch out	wear off

> *War <u>broke out</u> in September.*
> *You'll have to <u>stay up</u> late tonight.*

4 In the second structure, the verb is followed by a particle and an object.

fall for	feel for	grow on	look after
part with	pick on	set about	take after

> *She <u>looked after her invalid mother</u>.*
> *Peter <u>takes after his father</u> but John is more like me.*

5 In the third structure, the verb is followed by an object and a particle.

answer back	ask in	call back
catch out	count in	invite out
order about	tell apart	

> *I <u>answered him back</u> and took my chances.*
> *He loved to <u>order people about.</u>*

6 Some phrasal verbs can be used in both the second structure and the third structure: verb followed

by a particle and an object, or verb followed by an object and a particle.

add on	bring up	call up
fold up	hand over	knock over
point out	pull down	put away
put up	rub out	sort out
take up	tear up	throw away
try out		

It took ages to <u>clean up the mess.</u>
It took ages to <u>clean the mess up.</u>
There was such a mess. It took ages to <u>clean it up.</u>

WARNING: If the object is a pronoun, it must go in front of the particle. You cannot say 'He cleaned up it'.

7 In the fourth structure, the verb is followed by a particle and a preposition with an object.

break out of	catch up with
come down with	get on with
go down with	keep on at
look forward to	make off with
miss out on	play around with
put up with	run away with
stick up for	talk down to
walk out on	

Phrasal verbs

You go on ahead. I'll <u>catch up with</u> you later.
Children have to learn to <u>stick up for</u>
themselves.

8 A very few verbs are used in the structure: verb followed by an object, a particle, and a preposition with its object.

do out of	let in for	put down to
put up to	take out on	talk out of

I'll <u>take you up on</u> that generous invitation.
Kroop tried to <u>talk her out of</u> it.

Verbs and objects

Main points

Intransitive verbs do not have an object.

Transitive verbs have an object.

Some verbs can be used with or without an object, depending on the situation or their meaning.

1 Many verbs do not normally have an object. They are called 'intransitive' verbs. They often refer to:

existence:	appear die disappear happen live remain
the human body:	ache bleed blush faint shiver smile
human noises:	cough cry laugh scream snore speak yawn
light, smell, vibration:	glow shine sparkle stink throb vibrate
position, movement:	arrive come depart fall flow go kneel run sit sleep stand swim wait walk work

An awful thing <u>has happened.</u>

The girl <u>screamed.</u>
I <u>waited.</u>

Note that intransitive verbs cannot be used in the passive.

2 Many verbs normally have an object. These verbs are called 'transitive' verbs. They are often connected with:

physical objects:	build buy carry catch cover cut destroy hit own remove sell use waste wear
senses:	feel hear see smell taste touch
feelings:	admire enjoy fear frighten hate like love need prefer surprise trust want
facts, ideas:	accept believe correct discuss expect express forget include know mean remember report
people:	address blame comfort contact convince defy kill persuade please tease thank warn

He <u>hit the ball</u> really hard.
Did you <u>see the rainbow?</u>
They both <u>enjoyed the film.</u>
She <u>reported the accident</u> to the police.
Don't <u>blame me.</u>

Verbs and objects

Note that transitive verbs can be used in the passive.

They <u>were blamed</u> for everything.

🚫 WARNING: 'Have' is a transitive verb, but cannot be used in the passive. You can say 'I have a car' but not 'A car is had by me'.

3 Often, the people you are talking to know what the object is because of the situation, or because it has already been mentioned. In this case you can omit the object, even though the verb is transitive.

accept	answer	change	choose
clean	cook	draw	drive
eat	explain	forget	help
iron	know	learn	leave
paint	park	phone	read
remember	ride	sing	steal
study	type	understand	wash
watch	write		

I don't own a car. I can't <u>drive.</u>
You don't <u>smoke,</u> do you?
I asked a question and George <u>answered.</u>
Both dresses are beautiful. It's difficult to <u>choose.</u>

4 Many verbs have more than one meaning, and are transitive in one meaning and intransitive in another meaning. For example, the verb 'run' is intransitive

Verbs and objects

when you use it to mean 'move quickly' but transitive when you use it to mean 'manage or operate'.

call	fit	lose	manage	miss	move
play	run	show	spread		

> *The hare <u>runs</u> at enormous speed.*
> *She <u>runs a hotel.</u>*
> *She <u>moved</u> gracefully.*
> *The whole incident <u>had moved her</u> profoundly.*

5 A few verbs are normally intransitive, but can be used with an object that is closely related to the verb.

dance (a dance)	die (a death)	dream (a dream)
laugh (a laugh)	live (a life)	sigh (a sigh)
smile (a smile)		

> *Steve <u>smiled his thin, cruel smile.</u>*
> *He appears to have <u>lived the life of any other rich gentleman.</u>*
> *I once <u>dreamed a very nice dream.</u>*

Verbs with two objects

Main points

Some verbs have two objects, a direct object and an indirect object.

The indirect object can be used without a preposition, or after 'to' or 'for'.

1 Some verbs have two objects after them, a direct object and an indirect object. For example, in the sentence 'I gave John the book', 'the book' is the direct object. 'John' is the indirect object. Verbs that have two objects are sometimes called 'ditransitive' verbs or 'double-transitive' verbs.

> *His uncle had <u>given</u> him books on India.*
> *She <u>sends</u> you her love.*
> *I <u>passed</u> him the cup.*

2 When the indirect object is a pronoun, or another short noun group such as a noun with 'the', you put the indirect object in front of the direct object.

> *Dad gave <u>me</u> a car.*
> *You promised <u>the lad</u> a job.*

Verbs with two objects

> *He had lent <u>my cousin</u> the money.*
> *She bought <u>Dave and me</u> an ice cream.*

3 You can also use the prepositions 'to' and 'for' to introduce the indirect object. If you do this, you put the preposition and indirect object after the direct object.

> *Jonathon handed his room key <u>to the receptionist.</u>*
> *Bill saved the last piece of chocolate cake <u>for the children.</u>*

When the indirect object consists of several words, you normally use a preposition to introduce it.

> *She taught physics and chemistry <u>to pupils at the local school.</u>*
> *I made that lamp <u>for a seventy-year-old woman.</u>*

You often use a preposition when you want to emphasize the indirect object.

> *Did you really buy that <u>for me?</u>*
> *Give the book <u>to me!</u>*

4 With some verbs you can only use 'for', not 'to', to introduce the indirect object.

Verbs with two objects

book	buy	cook	cut	find
keep	make	paint	pour	prepare
save	win			

They booked a place <u>for me.</u>
My sister helped me find the money <u>for a private operation.</u>
The two children bought a present <u>for their teacher.</u>
She sat down and painted a picture <u>for her father.</u>

5 With some verbs you normally use 'to' to introduce the indirect object.

give	lend	offer	pass	pay	post
promise	read	sell	send	show	teach
tell					

I had lent my bicycle <u>to a friend.</u>
Ralph passed a message <u>to Jack.</u>
They told me they posted the letter <u>to me</u> last week.
He sold it <u>to me.</u>

Verbs with two objects

Note that you can use 'for' with these verbs, but it has a different meaning. 'For' indicates that one person does something on behalf of another person, so that the other person does not have to do it.

> *His mother paid the bill <u>for him.</u>*
> *If you're going out, can you post this <u>for me,</u> please?*

Reflexive verbs

Main points

Transitive verbs are used with a reflexive pronoun to indicate that the object is the same as the subject, for example: 'I hurt myself'.

Some verbs which do not normally have a person as the object can have reflexive pronouns as the object.

1 You use a reflexive pronoun after a transitive verb to indicate that the object is the same as the subject.

> *He blamed <u>himself</u> for his friend's death.*
> *I taught <u>myself</u> French.*
> *His comrades asked him if he had hurt <u>himself</u>.*

◆ See Unit 20 for more information on reflexive pronouns.

2 In theory, most transitive verbs can be used with a reflexive pronoun. However, you often use reflexive pronouns with the following verbs.

Reflexive verbs

amuse	blame	cut	dry
help	hurt	introduce	kill
prepare	repeat	restrict	satisfy
teach			

> *Sam <u>amused himself</u> by throwing branches into the fire.*
> *'Please can I borrow a pencil?' – 'Yes, <u>help yourself.</u>'*
> *<u>Prepare yourself</u> for a shock.*
> *He <u>introduced himself</u> to me.*

3 Verbs like 'dress', 'shave', and 'wash', which describe actions that people do to themselves, do not usually take reflexive pronouns in English, although they do in some other languages. With these verbs, reflexive pronouns are only used for emphasis.

> *I usually <u>shave</u> before breakfast.*
> *He prefers to <u>shave himself,</u> even with that broken arm.*
> *She <u>washed</u> very quickly and rushed downstairs.*
> *The children were encouraged to <u>wash themselves.</u>*

4 'Behave' does not normally take an object at all, but can take a reflexive pronoun as the object.

> If they don't <u>behave,</u> send them straight up to bed.
> He is old enough to know how to <u>behave himself.</u>

5 Some verbs do not normally have a person as the object, because they describe actions that you do not do to other people. However, these verbs can have reflexive pronouns as the object, because you can do these actions to yourself.

| apply | compose | distance | enjoy |
| excel | exert | express | strain |

> I really <u>enjoyed</u> the party.
> Just go out there, have a good time, and <u>enjoy yourself.</u>
> She <u>expressed</u> surprise at the news that he had returned.
> Professor Dale <u>expressed himself</u> very forcibly indeed.

Reflexive verbs

6 When 'busy' and 'content' are used as verbs, they always take a reflexive pronoun as their direct object. They are therefore true 'reflexive verbs'.

> *He had <u>busied himself</u> in the laboratory.*
> *I had to <u>content myself</u> with watching the little moving lights.*

Reciprocal verbs

Main points

Some verbs describe two people or two groups of people doing the same thing to each other, for example: 'We met', 'I met you', 'We met each other'.

You use 'each other' or 'one another' for emphasis.

With some verbs, you use 'each other' or 'one another' after 'with'.

1 Some verbs refer to actions that involve two people or two groups of people doing the same thing to each other. These verbs are sometimes called 'reciprocal' verbs.

> *We met in Delhi.*
> *Jane and Sarah told me that they met you.*
> *They met each other for the very first time last week.*

2 The two people or groups of people involved in the action are often mentioned as the plural subject of the verb, and the verb does not have an object. For

Reciprocal verbs

example, 'John and Mary argued' means that John argued with Mary and Mary argued with John.

argue	clash	coincide	combine
compete	fight	kiss	marry
match	meet		

The pair of you <u>have argued</u> about that for years.
We <u>competed</u> furiously.
Their children <u>are always fighting.</u>
They <u>kissed.</u>

3 When you want to emphasize that both people or groups of people are equally involved, you can use the pronouns 'each other' or 'one another' as the object of the verb. Verbs that refer to actions in which there is physical contact between people are often used with 'each other' or 'one another'.

cuddle	embrace	fight	hug	kiss	touch

We embraced <u>each other.</u>
They fought <u>one another</u> desperately for it.
They kissed <u>each other</u> in greeting.
It was the first time they had touched <u>one another.</u>

4 Some verbs do not take an object, so you use a preposition before 'each other' or 'one another'.

> They <u>parted from each other</u> after only two weeks.
> We <u>talk to one another</u> as often as possible.

5 With some verbs you have a choice of preposition before 'each other' or 'one another'. For example, you can 'fight with' one another or 'fight against' one another.

with/against:	compete fight
with/from:	part
with/to:	correspond relate talk

> Many countries are <u>competing with each other.</u>
> Did you <u>compete against each other</u> in yesterday's race?
> Stephen and I <u>parted with one another</u> on good terms.
> They <u>parted from one another</u> quite suddenly.

6 With some verbs, you can only use 'with' before 'each other' or 'one another'.

Note that most of these verbs refer to people talking or working together.

agree	argue	clash	collide
communicate	co-operate	disagree	quarrel

Reciprocal verbs

We do <u>agree with each other</u> sometimes.
Have they <u>communicated with each other</u> since then?
The two lorries <u>collided with one another</u> on the motorway.

7 If you want to focus on one of the people involved, you make them the subject of the verb and make the other person the object.

<u>She</u> married <u>a young engineer.</u>
<u>You</u> could meet <u>me</u> at the restaurant.

If the verb cannot take an object, you mention the other person after a preposition.

Youths clashed <u>with police</u> in Belfast.
She was always quarrelling <u>with him.</u>

Ergative verbs

Main points

Ergative verbs are both transitive and intransitive. The object of the transitive use is the subject of the intransitive use, for example: 'I opened the door'; 'The door opened'.

A few verbs are only ergative with particular nouns.

A few of these verbs need an adverbial when they are used without an object.

1. Some verbs can be used as transitive verbs to focus on the person who performs an action, and as intransitive verbs to focus on the thing affected by the action.

> When *I opened the door,* standing there was Laverne.
> Suddenly *the door opened.*

Note that the object of the transitive verb, in this case 'the door', is the subject of the intransitive verb. Verbs like these are called 'ergative' verbs.

2. Ergative verbs often refer to:

Ergative verbs

● changes

begin	break	change	crack
dry	end	finish	grow
improve	increase	slow	start
stop	tear		

I <u>broke</u> the glass.
The glass <u>broke</u> all over the floor.
The driver <u>stopped</u> the car.
A big car <u>stopped</u>.

● cooking

bake	boil	cook	defrost	fry	melt
roast	simmer				

I'<u>ve boiled</u> an egg.
The porridge <u>is boiling</u>.
I'<u>m cooking</u> spaghetti.
The rice <u>is cooking</u>.

● position or movement

balance	close	drop	move	open
rest	rock	shake	stand	turn

She <u>rested</u> her head on his shoulder.
Her head <u>rested</u> on the table.
An explosion <u>shook</u> the hotel.
The whole room <u>shook</u>.

Ergative verbs

● vehicles

back	crash	drive	fly	reverse	run	sail

> He <u>had crashed</u> the car twice.
> Her car <u>crashed</u> into a tree.
> She <u>sailed</u> her yacht round the world.
> The ship <u>sailed</u> on Monday.

3 Some verbs can be used in these two ways only with a small set of nouns. For example, you can say 'He fired a gun' or 'The gun fired'. You can do the same with other words referring to types of gun, 'cannon', 'pistol', or 'rifle'. However, although you can say 'He fired a bullet', you cannot say 'The bullet fired'.

catch:	belt, cloth, clothing, dress, shirt, trousers
fire:	cannon, gun, pistol, rifle
play:	guitar, music, piano, violin
ring:	alarm, bell
show:	anger, disappointment, emotions, fear, joy
sound:	alarm, bell, horn

> I <u>caught</u> my dress on the fence.
> My tights <u>caught</u> on a nail.
> A car <u>was sounding</u> its horn.
> A horn <u>sounded</u> in the night.

Ergative verbs

4 A few verbs can be used in both ways, but need an adverbial when they are used without an object.

clean	freeze	handle	mark
polish	sell	stain	wash

He <u>sells</u> books.
This book <u>is selling well.</u>
She <u>had handled</u> a machine gun.
This car <u>handles very nicely.</u>

Common verb + noun patterns

Main points

Examples are: 'have a bath'; 'give a shout'; 'make promises'; 'take care'.

Common verbs are often used with nouns to describe actions.

You use 'have' with nouns referring to eating, drinking, talking, and washing.

You use 'give' with nouns referring to noises, hitting, and talking.

You use 'make' with nouns referring to talking, plans, and travelling.

---

1 When you want to talk about actions, you often use common verbs with nouns as their object. The nouns describe the action. For example, if you say 'I had a shower', the noun tells you what the action was. The common verbs have very little meaning.

> I <u>had a nice rest.</u>
> She <u>made a remark</u> about the weather.

The nouns often have related verbs that do not take an object.

> *Helen went upstairs to <u>rest</u>.*
> *I <u>remarked</u> that it would be better if I came.*

2 Different verbs are used with different nouns.
You use 'have' with nouns referring to:

meals:	breakfast dinner drink lunch meal taste tea
talking:	chat conversation discussion talk
washing:	bath shower wash
relaxation:	break holiday rest
disagreement:	argument fight quarrel trouble

> *We usually <u>have lunch</u> at one o'clock.*
> *He was <u>having his first holiday</u> for five years.*

3 You use 'give' with nouns referring to:

human noises:	cry gasp giggle groan laugh scream shout sigh whistle yell
facial expressions:	grin smile
hitting:	kick punch push slap
talking:	advice answer example information interview lecture news report speech talk warning

> *Mr Sutton <u>gave a shout</u> of triumph.*
> *She <u>gave a long lecture</u> about Roosevelt.*

4 You use 'make' with nouns referring to:

talking and sounds:	comment enquiry noise point promise remark sound speech suggestion
plans:	arrangement choice decision plan
travelling:	journey tour trip visit

> *He <u>made the shortest speech</u> I've ever heard.*
> *In 1978 he <u>made his first visit</u> to Australia.*

5 You use 'take' with these nouns:

care	chance	charge
decision	interest	offence
photograph	responsibility	risk
time	trouble	turns

> *He was <u>taking no chances.</u>*
> *She was prepared to <u>take great risks.</u>*

6 You use 'go' and 'come' with '-ing' nouns referring to sports and outdoor activities.

> *She <u>goes climbing</u> in her holidays.*
> *Every morning, he <u>goes jogging</u> with Tommy.*

Note that you can also use 'go for' and 'come for' with 'a jog', 'a run', 'a swim', 'a walk'.

Common verb + noun patterns

They <u>went for a run</u> before breakfast.
Would you like to <u>come for a walk</u> with me?

7 You use 'do' with '-ing' nouns referring to jobs connected with the home, and nouns referring generally to work.

He wants to <u>do the cooking.</u>
He <u>does all the shopping</u> and I <u>do the washing.</u>
The man who <u>did the job</u> had ten years' training.
He has to get up early and <u>do a hard day's work.</u>

'Do' is often used instead of more specific verbs. For example, you can say 'Have you done your teeth?' instead of 'Have you brushed your teeth?'

Do I need to <u>do my hair?</u>

Auxiliary verbs

Main points

The auxiliaries 'be', 'have', and 'do' are used in forming tenses, negatives, and questions.

The auxiliary 'be' is used in forming the continuous tenses and the passive.

The auxiliary 'have' is used in forming the perfect tenses.

The auxiliary 'do' is used in making negative and question forms from sentences that have a verb in a simple tense.

1 The auxiliary verbs are 'be', 'have', and 'do'. They are used with a main verb to form tenses, negatives, and questions.

> *He __is__ planning to get married soon.*
> *I __haven't__ seen Peter since last night.*
> *Which doctor __do__ you want to see?*

2 'Be' as an auxiliary is used:

● with the '-ing' form of the main verb to form continuous tenses

> *He __is__ living in Germany.*
> *They __were__ going to phone you.*

Auxiliary verbs

● with the past participle of the main verb to form the passive

> *These cars <u>are</u> made in Japan.*
> *The walls of her flat <u>were</u> covered with posters.*

3 You use 'have' as an auxiliary with the past participle to form the perfect tenses.

> *I <u>have</u> changed my mind.*
> *I wish you <u>had</u> met Guy.*

The present perfect continuous, the past perfect continuous, and the perfect tenses in the passive, are formed using both 'have' and 'be'.

> *He <u>has been</u> working very hard recently.*
> *She did not know how long she <u>had been</u> lying there.*
> *The guest-room window <u>has been</u> mended.*
> *They <u>had been</u> taught by a young teacher.*

4 'Be' and 'have' are also used as auxiliaries in negative sentences and questions in continuous and perfect tenses, and in the passive.

> *He <u>isn't</u> going.*
> *<u>Hasn't</u> she seen it yet?*
> *<u>Was</u> it written in English?*

You use 'do' as an auxiliary to make negative and question forms from sentences that have a verb in the present simple or past simple.

> *He <u>doesn't</u> think he can come to the party.*
> *<u>Do</u> you like her new haircut?*
> *She <u>didn't</u> buy the house.*
> *<u>Didn't</u> he get the job?*

Note that you can use 'do' as a main verb with the auxiliary 'do'.

> *He <u>didn't do</u> his homework.*
> *<u>Do</u> they <u>do</u> the work themselves?*

You can also use the auxiliary 'do' with 'have' as a main verb.

> *He <u>doesn't have</u> any money.*
> *<u>Does</u> anyone <u>have</u> a question?*

You only use 'do' in affirmative sentences for emphasis or contrast.

> *I <u>do</u> feel sorry for Roger.*

⊖ WARNING: You never use the auxiliary 'do' with 'be' except in the imperative.

> *<u>Don't be</u> stupid!*
> *<u>Do be</u> a good boy and sit still.*

5 Some grammars include modals among the auxiliary verbs. When there is a modal in the verb group, it is always the first word in the verb group, and comes before the auxiliaries 'be' and 'have'.

234

Auxiliary verbs

> *She <u>might be</u> going to Switzerland for*
> *Christmas.*
> *I <u>would have</u> liked to have seen her.*

Note that you never use the auxiliary 'do' with a modal.

➤ See Units 79-91 for more information on modals.

The present tenses

Main points

There are four present tenses – present simple ('I walk'), present continuous ('I am walking'), present perfect ('I have walked'), and present perfect continuous ('I have been walking').

All the present tenses are used to refer to a time which includes the present.

Present tenses can also be used for predictions made in the present about future events.

1 There are four tenses which begin with a verb in the present tense. They are the present simple, the present continuous, the present perfect, and the present perfect continuous. These are the present tenses.

2 The present simple and the present continuous are used with reference to present time. If you are talking about the general present, or about a regular or habitual action, you use the present simple.

The present tenses

George <u>lives</u> in Birmingham.
They often <u>phone</u> my mother in London.

If you are talking about something in the present situation, you use the present continuous.

He'<u>s playing</u> tennis at the University.
I'<u>m cooking</u> the dinner.

The present continuous is often used to refer to a temporary situation.

She'<u>s living</u> in a flat at present.

3 You use the present perfect or the present perfect continuous when you are concerned with the present effects of something which happened at a time in the past, or which started in the past but is still continuing.

<u>Have</u> you <u>seen</u> the film at the Odeon?
We'<u>ve been waiting</u> here since before two o'clock.

4 If you are talking about something which is scheduled or timetabled to happen in the future, you can use the present simple tense.

The next train <u>leaves</u> at two fifteen in the morning.
It'<u>s</u> Tuesday tomorrow.

5. If you are talking about something which has been arranged for the future, you can use the present continuous. When you use the present continuous like this, there is nearly always a time adverbial like 'tomorrow', 'next week', or 'later' in the clause.

> We're going on holiday with my parents this year.
> The Browns are having a birthday party next week.
> Later on I'm speaking to Patty.

6. It is only in the main clauses that the choice of tense can be related to a particular time. In sub-ordinate clauses, for example in 'if'– clauses, time clauses, and defining relative clauses, present tenses often refer to a future time in relation to the time in the main clause.

> You can go at eleven thirty if you have finished.
> Let's have something to eat and drink before we start.
> We'll save some food for anyone who arrives late.

The present tenses

7 The present simple tense normally has no auxiliary verb, but questions and negative sentences are formed with the auxiliary 'do'.

> _Do_ you _live_ round here?
> _Does_ your husband _do_ most of the cooking?
> They _don't_ often _phone_ during the week.
> She _doesn't like_ being late if she can help it.

The past tenses

Main points

There are four past tenses – past simple ('I walked'), past continuous ('I was walking'), past perfect ('I had walked'), and past perfect continuous ('I had been walking').

All the past tenses are used to refer to past time.

The past tenses are often used as polite forms.

The past tenses have special meanings in conditional clauses and when referring to imaginary situations.

1 There are four tenses which begin with a verb in the past tense. They are the past simple, the past continuous, the past perfect, and the past perfect continuous. These are the past tenses. They are used to refer to past time, and also to refer to imaginary situations, and to express politeness.

2 The past simple and the past continuous are used with reference to past time. You use the past simple for events which happened in the past.

The past tenses

I <u>woke up</u> early and <u>got</u> out of bed.
I <u>caught</u> my dress on the fence.

If you are talking about the general past, or about regular or habitual actions in the past, you also use the past simple.

She <u>lived</u> just outside London.
We often <u>saw</u> his dog sitting outside his house.

If you are talking about something which continued to happen before and after a particular time in the past, you use the past continuous.

They <u>were sitting</u> in the kitchen, when they heard the explosion.
Jack arrived while the children <u>were having</u> their bath.

The past continuous is often used to refer to a temporary situation.

He <u>was working</u> at home at the time.
Bill <u>was using</u> my office until I came back from America.

3 You use the past perfect and past perfect continuous tenses when you are talking about the past and you are concerned with something which happened at an earlier time, or which had started at an earlier time but was still continuing.

> *I <u>had heard</u> it was a good film so we decided to go and see it.*
> *It was getting late. I <u>had been waiting</u> there since two o'clock.*

4 You sometimes use a past tense rather than a present tense when you want to be more polite. For example, in the following pairs of sentences, the second one is more polite.

> *<u>Do</u> you <u>want</u> to see me now?*
> *<u>Did</u> you <u>want</u> to see me now?*
> *I <u>wonder</u> if you can help me.*
> *I <u>was wondering</u> if you could help me.*

5 The past tenses have special meanings in conditional clauses and when referring to hypothetical and imaginary situations, for example after 'I wish' or 'What if…?'. You use the past simple and past continuous for something that you think is unlikely to happen.

> *If they <u>saw</u> the mess, they would be extremely angry.*
> *We would certainly tell you if we <u>were selling</u> the house.*
> *What if you <u>asked</u> her for the money instead?*

The past tenses

You use the past perfect and past perfect continuous when you are talking about something which could have happened in the past, but which did not actually happen.

> *If I <u>had known</u> that you were coming, I would have told Jim.*
> *They wouldn't have gone to bed if they <u>had been expecting</u> you to arrive.*

The continuous tenses

Main points

Continuous tenses describe actions which continue to happen before and after a particular time.

Continuous tenses can also indicate duration and change.

1. You use a continuous tense to indicate that an action continues to happen before and after a particular time, without stopping. You use the present continuous for actions which continue to happen before and after the moment of speaking.

> I'm looking at the photos my brother sent me.
> They're having a meeting.

2. When you are talking about two actions in the present tense, you use the present continuous for an action that continues to happen before and after another action that interrupts it. You use the present simple for the other action.

> The phone always rings when I'm having a bath.
> Friends always talk to me when I'm trying to study.

The continuous tenses

Unit 60

3 When you are talking about the past, you use the past continuous for actions that continued to happen before and after another action, or before and after a particular time. This is often called the 'interrupted past'. You use the past simple for the other action.

> He _was watching_ television when the doorbell rang.
> It was 6 o'clock. The train _was nearing_ London.

⊖ WARNING: If two things happened one after another, you use two verbs in the past simple tense.

> As soon as he _saw_ me, he _waved._

4 You can use continuous forms with modals in all their usual meanings.

➤ See Units 79 to 91 for more information on modals.

> What _could_ he _be thinking_ of?
> They _might be telling_ lies.

5 You use continuous tenses to express duration, when you want to emphasize how long something has been happening or will happen for.

> We _had been living_ in Athens for five years.
> They'_ll be staying_ with us for a couple of weeks.

The continuous tenses

> He *has been building up* the business all his life.
> By 1992, he *will have been working* for ten
> years.

Note that you do not have to use continuous tenses for duration.

> We *had lived* in Africa for five years.
> He *worked* for us for ten years.

6 You use continuous tenses to describe a state or situation that is temporary.

> I'*m living* in London at the moment.
> He'*ll be working* nights next week.
> She'*s spending* the summer in Europe.

7 You use continuous tenses to show that something is changing, developing, or progressing.

> Her English *was improving.*
> The children *are growing up* quickly.
> The video industry *has been developing* rapidly.

8 As a general rule, verbs which refer to actions that require a deliberate effort can be used in continuous tenses, verbs which refer to actions that do not require a deliberate effort are not used in continuous tenses.

> I *think* it's going to rain. ('think' = 'believe'.
> Believing does not require deliberate effort)

The continuous tenses

Please be quiet. I'm thinking. ('think' = 'try to solve a problem'. Trying to solve a problem does require deliberate effort)

However, many verbs are not normally used in the continuous tenses. These include verbs that refer to thinking, liking and disliking, appearance, possession, and perception.

➤ See Unit 62 for lists of these verbs.

The perfect tenses

Main points

You use the present perfect ('I have walked') to relate the past to the present.

You use the past perfect ('I had walked') to talk about a situation that occurred before a particular time in the past.

1 You use the present perfect tense when you are concerned with the present effects of something which happened at an indefinite time in the past.

> *I'm afraid I've forgotten my book.*
> *Have you heard from Jill recently?*

Sometimes, the present effects are important because they are very recent.

> *Karen has just passed her exams.*

You also use the present perfect when you are thinking of a time which started in the past and is still continuing.

> *Have you really lived here for ten years?*
> *He has worked here since 1987.*

The perfect tenses

You also use the present perfect in time clauses, when you are talking about something which will be done at some time in the future.

> *Tell me when you <u>have finished</u>.*
> *I'll write to you as soon as I <u>have heard</u> from Jenny.*

2 When you want to emphasize the fact that a recent event continued to happen for some time, you use the present perfect continuous.

> *She'<u>s been crying</u>.*
> *I'<u>ve been working</u> hard all day.*

3 You use the past perfect tense when you are looking back from a point in past time, and you are concerned with the effects of something which happened at an earlier time in the past.

> *I apologized because I <u>had forgotten</u> my book again.*
> *He felt much happier once he <u>had found</u> a new job.*
> *Mr and Mrs Jones would have come if we <u>had invited</u> them.*

You also use the past perfect when you are thinking of a time which had started earlier in the past but was still continuing.

The perfect tenses

> *I was about twenty. I <u>had been studying</u> French for a couple of years.*
> *He hated games and <u>had always managed</u> to avoid children's parties.*

4 You use the future perfect tense when you are looking back from a point in the future and you are talking about something which will have happened at a time between now and that future point.

> *In another two years, you <u>will have left</u> school.*
> *Take these tablets, and in twenty-four hours the pain <u>will have gone.</u>*

You also use the future perfect when you are looking back from the present and guessing that an action will be finished.

> *I'm sure they <u>will have arrived</u> at the airport by now.*
> *It's too late to ring Don. He <u>will have left</u> the house by now.*

5 You can also use other modals with 'have', when you are looking back from a point in time at something which you think may have happened at an earlier time.

The perfect tenses

I <u>might have finished</u> work by then.
He <u>should have arrived</u> in Paris by the time we phone.

➤ For more information on modals with 'have', see Units 79 to 91.

Talking about the present

Main points

For the general present, general truths, and habitual actions, you use the present simple ('I walk').

For something which is happening now, or for temporary situations, you use the present continuous ('I am walking').

1. If you are talking about the present in general, you normally use the present simple tense. You use the present simple for talking about the general present including the present moment.

> *My dad <u>works</u> in Saudi Arabia.*
> *He <u>lives</u> in the French Alps near the Swiss border.*

2. If you are talking about general truths, you use the present simple.

> *Water <u>boils</u> at 100 degrees centigrade.*
> *Love <u>makes</u> the world go round.*
> *The bus <u>takes</u> longer than the train.*

Talking about the present

3 If you are talking about regular or habitual actions, you use the present simple.

> *Do you eat meat?*
> *I get up early and eat my breakfast in bed.*
> *I pay the milkman on Fridays.*

4 If you are talking about something which is regarded as temporary, you use the present continuous tense.

> *Do you know if she's still playing tennis these days?*
> *I'm working as a British Council officer.*

5 If you are talking about something which is happening now, you normally use the present continuous tense.

> *We're having a meeting. Come and join in.*
> *Wait a moment. I'm listening to the news.*

6 There are a number of verbs which are used in the present simple tense even when you are talking about the present moment. These verbs are not normally used in the present continuous or the other continuous tenses.

Talking about the present

These verbs usually refer to:

thinking:	believe forget imagine know realize recognize suppose think understand want wish
liking and disliking:	admire dislike hate like love prefer
appearance:	appear look like resemble seem
possession:	belong to contain have include own possess
perception:	hear see smell taste
being:	be consist of exist

> I *believe* he was not to blame.
> She *hates* going to parties.
> Our neighbours *have* two cars.

Note that you normally use verbs of perception with the modal 'can', rather than using the present simple tense.

> I *can smell* gas.

Some other common verbs are not normally used in the present continuous or the other continuous tenses.

Talking about the present

concern	deserve	fit	interest	involve
matter	mean	satisfy	surprise	

What <u>do</u> you <u>mean</u>?

⊖ WARNING: Some of the verbs listed above can be used in continuous tenses in other meanings. For example, 'have' referring to possession is not used in continuous tenses. You do not say 'I am having a car'. But note the following examples.

We'<u>re having</u> a party tomorrow.
He'<u>s having</u> problems with his car.
She'<u>s having</u> a shower.

Talking about the past

Main points

For actions, situations, or regular events in the past, you use the past simple ('I walked'). For regular events in the past, you can also use 'would' or 'used to'.

For events that happened before and after a time in the past, and for temporary situations, you use the past continuous ('I was walking').

For present effects of past situations, you use the present perfect ('I have walked'), and for past effects of earlier events you use the past perfect ('I had walked').

For future in the past, you use 'would', 'was/were going to', or the past continuous ('I was walking').

1 When you want to talk about an event that occurred at a particular time in the past, you use the past simple.

> *The Prime Minister <u>flew</u> into New York yesterday.*
> *The new term <u>started</u> last week.*

You also use the past simple to talk about a situation that existed over a period of time in the past.

Talking about the past

> *We <u>spent</u> most of our time at home last winter.*
> *They <u>earned</u> their money quickly that year.*

2 When you want to talk about something which took place regularly in the past, you use the past simple.

> *They <u>went</u> for picnics most weekends.*
> *We usually <u>spent</u> the winter at Aunt Meg's house.*

⊖ WARNING: The past simple always refers to a time in the past. A time reference is necessary to say what time in the past you are referring to. The time reference can be established in an earlier sentence or by another speaker, but it must be established.

When you want to talk about something which occurred regularly in the past, you can use 'would' or 'used to' instead of the past simple.

> *We <u>would</u> normally <u>spend</u> the winter in Miami.*
> *People <u>used to believe</u> that the world was flat.*

⊖ WARNING: You do not normally use 'would' with this meaning with verbs which are not used in the continuous tenses.

➤ For a list of these verbs, see Unit 62.

3 When you want to talk about something which continued to happen before and after a given time

Talking about the past

in the past, you use the past continuous.

> *I hurt myself when I <u>was mending</u> my bike.*
> *It was midnight. She <u>was driving</u> home.*

You also use the past continuous to talk about a temporary state of affairs in the past.

> *Our team <u>were losing</u> 2-1 at the time.*
> *We <u>were staying</u> with friends in Italy.*

➤ For more information on continuous tenses, see Unit 60.

4 When you are concerned with the present effects or future effects of something which happened at an indefinite time in the past, you use the present perfect.

> *I'm afraid I'<u>ve forgotten</u> my book, so I don't know.*
> *<u>Have</u> you <u>heard</u> from Jill recently? How is she?*

You also use the present perfect when you are thinking of a time which started in the past and still continues.

> *<u>Have</u> you ever <u>stolen</u> anything?* (= at any time up to the present)
> *He <u>has been</u> here since six o'clock.* (= and he is still here)

Talking about the past

5 When you are looking back from a point in past time, and you are concerned with the effects of something which happened at an earlier time in the past, you use the past perfect.

> *I apologized because I <u>had left</u> my wallet at home.*
> *They would have come if we <u>had invited</u> them.*

6 When you want to talk about the future from a point of view in past time, you can use 'would', 'was / were going to', or the past continuous.

> *He thought to himself how wonderful it <u>would taste.</u>*
> *Her daughter <u>was going to</u> do the cooking.*
> *Mike <u>was taking</u> his test the week after.*

Main points

When you are making predictions about the future or talking about future intentions, you can use either 'will' ('I will walk') or 'going to' ('I am going to walk').

For promises and offers relating to the future, you use 'will' ('I will walk').

For future events based on arrangements, you use the future continuous ('I will be walking').

For events that will happen before a time in the future, you use the future perfect ('I will have walked').

1 You cannot talk about the future with as much certainty as you can about the present or the past. You are usually talking about what you think might happen or what you intend to happen. This is why you often use modals. Although most modals can be used with future reference, you most often use the modal 'will' to talk about the future.

> Nancy <u>will arrange</u> it.
> When <u>will</u> I <u>see</u> them?

'Will' and 'going to'

2. When you are making predictions about the future that are based on general beliefs, opinions, or attitudes, you use 'will'.

> *The weather tomorrow <u>will be</u> warm and sunny.*
> *I'm sure you <u>will enjoy</u> your visit to the zoo.*

This use of 'will' is common in sentences with conditional clauses.

> *You'<u>ll be</u> late, if you don't hurry.*

When you are using facts or events in the present situation as evidence for a prediction, you can use 'going to'.

> *It'<u>s going to rain.</u> (I can see black clouds)*
> *I'<u>m going to be late.</u> (I have missed my train)*

3. When you are talking about your own intentions, you use 'will' or 'going to'.

> *I'<u>ll ring you</u> tonight.*
> *I'<u>m going to stay</u> at home today.*

When you are saying what someone else has decided to do, you use 'going to'.

> *They'<u>re going to have</u> a party.*
> *She'<u>s going to be</u> an actress.*

'Will' and 'going to'

⊖ WARNING: You do not normally use 'going to' with the verb 'go'. You usually just say 'I'm going' rather than 'I'm going to go'.

> 'What <u>are you going to do</u> this weekend?' – 'I'<u>m going</u> to the cinema.'

When you are announcing a decision you have just made or are about to make, you use 'will'.

> I'm tired. I think I'<u>ll go</u> to bed.

4 In promises and offers relating to the future, you often use 'will' with the meaning 'be willing to'.

> I'<u>ll do</u> what I can.
> I'<u>ll help</u> with the washing-up.

Note that you can use 'will' with this meaning in an 'if'-clause.

> I'll put you through, if you'<u>ll hang on</u> for a minute. (= if you are willing to hang on for a minute)

⊖ WARNING: Remember that you do not normally use 'will' in 'if'-clauses.

▶ See Unit 66 for more information on 'if'-clauses.

> If you <u>do</u> that, you will be wasting your time.
> The children will call out if they <u>think</u> he is wrong.

'Will' and 'going to'

5 When you want to say that something will happen because arrangements have been made, you use the future continuous tense.

> I'<u>ll be seeing</u> them when I've finished with you.
> I'<u>ll be waiting</u> for you outside.
> She'<u>ll be appearing</u> at the Royal Festival Hall.

6 When you want to talk about something that has not happened yet but will happen before a particular time in the future, you use the future perfect tense.

> By the time we phone he'<u>ll</u> already <u>have started.</u>
> By 2010, he <u>will have worked</u> for twelve years.

Present tenses for future

Main points

When you are talking about the future in relation to official timetables or the calendar, you use the present simple ('I walk').

When talking about people's plans and arrangements for the future, you use the present continuous ('I am walking').

In 'if'-clauses, time clauses, and defining relative clauses, you can use the present simple ('I walk') to refer to the future.

1 When you are talking about something in the future which is based on an official time-table or calendar, you use the present simple tense. You usually put a time adverbial in these sentences.

> My last train _leaves_ Euston _at 11.30_ on Tuesday morning.
> The UN General Assembly _opens_ in New York _this month._
> Our next lesson _is on Thursday._
> We _set off early tomorrow morning._

Present tenses for future

2 In statements about fixed dates, you normally use the present simple.

> *Tomorrow <u>is</u> Tuesday.*
> *It'<u>s</u> my birthday next month.*
> *Monday <u>is</u> the seventeenth of July.*

3 When you want to talk about people's plans or arrangements for the future, you use the present continuous tense.

> *I'<u>m meeting</u> Bill next week.*
> *They'<u>re getting married</u> in June.*
> *We'<u>re going</u> to Barbados at the beginning of September.*

4 You often talk about the future using the present tense of verbs such as 'hope', 'expect', 'intend', and 'want' with a 'to'-infinitive clause, especially when you want to indicate your uncertainty about what will actually happen.

> *We <u>hope to see</u> you soon.*
> *Bill <u>expects to be</u> back at work tomorrow morning.*
> *They <u>intend to press ahead</u> with plans to scrap the current system.*

Present tenses for future

After the verb 'hope', you often use the present simple to refer to the future.

> *I hope you <u>enjoy</u> your holiday.*

5 In subordinate clauses, the relationships between tense and time are different. In 'if'-clauses and time clauses, you normally use the present simple for future reference.

> *If he <u>comes</u>, I'll let you know.*
> *Please start when you <u>are</u> ready.*
> *We won't start the meeting until everyone <u>arrives</u>.*
> *Don't forget to lock the door after you finally <u>leave</u>.*

6 In defining relative clauses, you normally use the present simple, not 'will', to refer to the future.

> *Any decision <u>that you make</u> will need her approval.*
> *Give my love to any friends <u>you meet</u> at the party.*
> *There is a silver cup for the runner <u>who finishes first</u>.*

Present tenses for future

7 If you want to show that a condition has to be the case before an action can be carried out, you use the present perfect for future events.

> *We won't start until everyone <u>has arrived.</u>*
> *I'll let you know when I <u>have arranged</u> everything.*

Conditionals using 'if'

Main points

You use conditional clauses to talk about a possible situation and its results.

Conditional clauses can begin with 'if'.

A conditional clause needs a main clause to make a complete sentence. The conditional clause can come before or after the main clause.

1 You use conditional clauses to talk about a situation that might possibly happen and to say what its results might be.

You use 'if' to mention events and situations that happen often, that may happen in the future, that could have happened in the past but did not happen, or that are unlikely to happen at all.

> _If_ the light comes on, the battery is OK.
> I'll call you _if_ I need you.
> _If_ I had known, I'd have told you.
> _If_ she asked me, I'd help her.

2 When you are talking about something that is generally true or happens often, you use a present or

Conditionals using 'if'

present perfect tense in the main clause and the conditional clause.

> *If they <u>lose</u> weight during an illness, they soon <u>regain</u> it afterwards.*
> *If an advertisement <u>does not tell</u> the truth, the advertiser <u>is committing</u> an offence.*
> *If the baby <u>is crying,</u> it <u>is</u> probably hungry.*
> *If they <u>have lost</u> any money, they <u>report</u> it to me.*

⊖ WARNING: You do not use the present continuous in both clauses. You do not say 'If they are losing money, they are getting angry.'

3 When you use a conditional clause with a present or present perfect tense, you often use an imperative in the main clause.

> *<u>Wake</u> me <u>up</u> if you're worried.*
> *If he has finished, <u>ask</u> him to leave quietly.*
> *If you are very early, <u>don't expect</u> them to be ready.*

4 When you are talking about something which may possibly happen in the future, you use a present or present perfect tense in the conditional clause, and the simple future in the main clause.

> *If I <u>marry</u> Celia, we <u>will need</u> the money.*

Conditionals using 'if'

> *If you <u>are going</u> to America, you <u>will need</u> a visa.*
>
> *If he <u>has done</u> the windows, he <u>will want</u> his money.*

⊖ WARNING: You do not normally use 'will' in conditional clauses. You do not say 'If I will see you tomorrow, I will give you the book'.

5 When you are talking about something that you think is unlikely to happen, you use the past simple or past continuous in the conditional clause and 'would' in the main clause.

> *If I <u>had</u> enough money, I <u>would buy</u> the car.*
>
> *If he <u>was coming</u>, he <u>would ring</u>.*

⊖ WARNING: You do not normally use 'would' in conditional clauses. You do not say 'If I would do it, I would do it like this'.

6 'Were' is sometimes used instead of 'was' in the conditional clause, especially after 'I'.

> *If I <u>were</u> as big as you, I would kill you.*
>
> *If I <u>weren't</u> so busy, I would do it for you.*

You often say 'If I were you' when you are giving someone advice.

Conditionals using 'if'

> *If I were you,* I would take the money.
> *I should keep out of Bernadette's way if I were*
> *you.*

7. When you are talking about something which could have happened in the past but which did not actually happen, you use the past perfect in the conditional clause. In the main clause, you use 'would have' and a past participle.

> *If he had realized that, he would have run*
> *away.*
> *I wouldn't have been so depressed if I had*
> *known how common this feeling is.*

⊖ WARNING: You do not use 'would have' in the conditional clause. You do not say 'If I would have seen him, I would have told him'.

'If' with modals; 'unless'

Main points

You can use a modal in a conditional clause.

You use 'unless' to mention an exception to what you are saying.

1. You sometimes use modals in conditional clauses. In the main clause, you can still use a present tense for events that happen often, 'will' for events that are quite likely in the future, 'would' for an event that is unlikely to happen, and 'would have' for events that were possible but did not happen.

> *If he <u>can't</u> come, he usually phones me.*
> *If they <u>must</u> have it today, they will have to come back at five o'clock.*
> *If I <u>could</u> only find the time, I'd do it gladly.*
> *If you <u>could</u> have seen him, you would have laughed too.*

'Should' is sometimes used in conditional clauses to express greater uncertainty.

> *If any visitors <u>should</u> come, I'll say you aren't here.*

'If' with modals; 'unless'

2 You can use other modals besides 'will', 'would' and 'would have' in the main clause with their usual meanings.

> She _might_ phone me, if she has time.
> You _could_ come, if you wanted to.
> If he sees you leaving, he _may_ cry.

Note that you can have modals in both clauses: the main clause and the conditional clause.

> If he _can't_ come, he _will_ phone.

▶ See Units 79 to 91 for more information.

3 In formal English, if the first verb in a conditional clause is 'had', 'should', or 'were', you can put the verb at the beginning of the clause and omit 'if'.

For example, instead of saying 'If he should come, I will tell him you are sick', it is possible to say 'Should he come, I will tell him you are sick'.

> _Should_ ministers decide to hold an inquiry, we would welcome it.
> _Were_ it all true, it would still not excuse their actions.
> _Had_ I known, I would not have done it.

4 When you want to mention an exception to what you are saying, you use a conditional clause beginning with 'unless'.

'If' with modals; 'unless'

> *You will fail your exams.*
> *You will fail your exams <u>unless you work harder.</u>*

Note that you can often use 'if...not' instead of 'unless'.

> *You will fail your exams <u>if</u> you do <u>not</u> work harder.*

When you use 'unless', you use the same tenses that you use with 'if'.

> *She <u>spends</u> Sundays in the garden unless the weather <u>is</u> awful.*
> *We usually <u>walk,</u> unless we'<u>re going</u> shopping.*
> *He <u>will</u> not <u>let</u> you go unless he <u>is forced</u> to do so.*
> *You <u>wouldn't believe</u> it, unless you <u>saw</u> it.*

5 'If' and 'unless' are not the only ways of beginning conditional clauses. You can also use 'as long as', 'only if', 'provided', 'provided that', 'providing', 'providing that', or 'so long as'. These expressions are all used to indicate that one thing only happens or is true if another thing happens or is true.

> *We were all right <u>as long as</u> we kept our heads down.*
> *I will come <u>only if</u> nothing is said to the press.*

She was prepared to come, <u>provided that</u> she could bring her daughter.

<u>Providing</u> they remained at a safe distance, we would be all right.

Detergent cannot harm a fabric, <u>so long as</u> it has been properly dissolved.

I wish, if only, …as if…

Main points

You use 'I wish' and 'If only' to talk about wishes and regrets.

You use '…as if…' and '…as though…' to show that information in a manner clause is not or might not be true.

1. You can express what you want to happen now by using 'I wish' or 'If only' followed by a past simple verb.

> *I wish* he *wasn't* here.
> *If only* she *had* a car.

Note that in formal English, you sometimes use 'were' instead of 'was' in sentences like these.

> *I* often *wish* that I *were* really wealthy.

When you want to express regret about past events, you use the past perfect.

> *I wish* I *hadn't married* him.

When you want to say that you wish that someone was able to do something, you use 'could'.

> *If only* they *could* come with us!

I wish, if only, …as if…

When you want to say that you wish that someone was willing to do something, you use 'would'.

> *If only they would realise how stupid they've been.*

2 When you want to indicate that the information in a manner clause might not be true, or is definitely not true, you use 'as if' or 'as though'.

> *She reacted as if she didn't know about the race.*
> *She acts as though she owns the place.*

After 'as if' or 'as though', you often use a past tense even when you are talking about the present, to emphasize that the information in the manner clause is not true. In formal English, you use 'were' instead of 'was'.

> *Presidents can't dispose of companies as if people didn't exist.*
> *She treats him as though he was her own son.*
> *He looked at me as though I were mad.*

3 You can also use 'as if' or 'as though' to say how someone or something feels, looks, or sounds.

> *She felt as if she had a fever.*
> *He looked as if he hadn't slept very much.*
> *Mary sounded as though she had just run all the way.*

I wish, if only, …as if…

You can also use 'it looks' and 'it sounds' with 'as if' and 'as though'.

> *It looks to me <u>as if</u> he wrote down some notes.*
> *It sounds to me <u>as though</u> he's just being awkward.*

4 When the subject of the manner clause and the main clause are the same, you can often use a participle in the manner clause and omit the subject and the verb 'be'.

> *He ran off to the house <u>as if escaping.</u>*
> *He shook his head <u>as though dazzled</u> by his own vision.*

You can also use 'as if' or 'as though' with a 'to'-infinitive clause.

> *<u>As if to remind</u> him, the church clock struck eleven.*

5 In informal speech, people often use 'like' instead of 'as if' or 'as' to say how a person feels, looks, or sounds. Some speakers of English think that this use of 'like' is incorrect.

> *He felt <u>like</u> he'd won the pools.*
> *You look <u>like</u> you've seen a ghost.*
> *You talk just <u>like</u> my father does.*

I wish, if only, ...as if...

You can also use 'like' in prepositional phrases to say how someone does something.

> *He was sleeping <u>like a baby.</u>*
> *I behaved <u>like an idiot</u>, and I'm sorry.*

Verbs with '-ing' clauses

Main points

Many verbs are followed by an '-ing' clause.

Some verbs are followed by an object and an '-ing' clause that describes what the object is doing.

1. Many verbs are followed by an '-ing' clause. The subject of the verb is also the subject of the '-ing' clause. The '-ing' clause begins with an '-ing' form. The most common of these verbs are:

● verbs of saying and thinking

| admit | consider | deny | describe |
| imagine | mention | recall | suggest |

> He _denied taking_ drugs.
> I _suggested meeting_ her for a coffee.

Note that all of these verbs except for 'describe' can also be followed by a 'that'-clause.

➤ See Unit 76.

> He _denied that_ he was involved.

Verbs with '-ing' clauses

● verbs of liking and disliking

adore	detest	dislike	dread	enjoy
fancy	like	love	mind	resent

> *Will they <u>enjoy using</u> it?*
> *I <u>don't mind telling</u> you.*

'Like' and 'love' can also be followed by a 'to'-infinitive clause.

➤ See Unit 71.

● other common verbs

avoid	commence	delay	finish
involve	keep	miss	postpone
practise	resist	risk	stop

> *I've just <u>finished reading</u> that book.*
> *<u>Avoid giving</u> any unnecessary information.*

● common phrasal verbs

burst out	carry on	end up	give up	go
round	keep on	put off	set about	

> *She <u>carried on reading</u>.*
> *They <u>kept on walking</u> for a while.*

Note that some common phrases can be followed by an '-ing' clause.

Verbs with '-ing' clauses

can't help	can't stand	feel like

I <u>can't help worrying.</u>

2 After the verbs and phrases mentioned above, you can also use 'being' followed by a past participle.

> *They enjoy <u>being praised.</u>*
> *I dislike <u>being interrupted.</u>*

After some verbs of saying and thinking, you can use 'having' followed by a past participle.

admit	deny	mention	recall

> *Michael <u>denied having seen</u> him.*

3 'Come' and 'go' are used with '-ing' clauses to describe the way that a person or thing moves.

> *They both <u>came running out.</u>*
> *It <u>went sliding</u> across the road out of control.*

'Go' and 'come' are also used with '-ing' nouns to talk about sports and outdoor activities. ➤ See Unit 56.

> *Did you say they might <u>go camping?</u>*

4 Some verbs can be followed by an object and an '-ing' clause. The object of the verb is the subject of the '-ing' clause.

Verds with '-ing' clauses

catch	find	imagine	leave
prevent	stop	watch	

> *It is hard <u>to imagine him existing</u> without it.*
> *He <u>left them making</u> their calculations.*

Note that 'prevent' and 'stop' are often used with 'from' in front of the '-ing' clause.

> *I wanted to <u>prevent him from seeing</u> that.*

Most verbs of perception can be followed by an object and an '-ing' clause or a base form.
➤ See Unit 72.

> *I <u>saw him riding</u> a bicycle.*
> *I <u>saw a policeman walk over</u> to one of them.*

➤ See also Unit 94 for '-ing' clauses after nouns.

Main points

Some verbs are followed by a 'to'-infinitive clause. Others are followed by an object and a 'to'-infinitive clause.

Some verbs are followed by a 'wh'-word and a 'to'-infinitive clause. Others are followed by an object, a 'wh'-word, and a 'to'-infinitive clause.

Nouns are followed by 'to'-infinitive clauses that indicate the aim, purpose or necessity of something, or that give extra information.

1 Some verbs are followed by a 'to'-infinitive clause. The subject of the verb is also the subject of the 'to'-infinitive clause.

● verbs of saying and thinking

agree	choose	decide	expect
hope	intend	learn	mean
offer	plan	promise	refuse

She had agreed to let us use her flat for a while.
I decided not to go out for the evening.

Infinitives

● other verbs

fail	manage	pretend	tend	want

England <u>failed to win</u> a place in the European finals.

2 Some verbs are followed by an object and a 'to'-infinitive clause. The object of the verb is the subject of the 'to'-infinitive clause.

● verbs of saying and thinking

advise	ask	encourage	expect
invite	order	persuade	remind
teach	tell		

I <u>asked her to explain.</u>
They <u>advised us not to wait around</u> too much longer.

● other verbs

allow	force	get	help	want

I could <u>get someone else to do</u> it.
I <u>didn't want him to go.</u>

Note that 'help' can also be followed by an object and a base form.

I <u>helped him fix</u> it.

Infinitives

⊖ WARNING: You do not use 'want' with a 'that'-clause. You do not say 'I want that you do something'.

3 Some verbs are followed by 'for' and an object, then a 'to'-infinitive clause. The object of 'for' is the subject of the 'to'-infinitive clause.

appeal	arrange	ask	long	pay	wait	wish

> *Could you <u>arrange for a taxi to collect</u> us?*
> *I <u>waited for him to speak.</u>*

4 Some link verbs, and 'pretend' are followed by 'to be' and an '-ing' form for continuing actions, and by 'to have' and a past participle for finished actions.
➤ See also Unit 73.

> *We <u>pretended to be looking</u> inside.*
> *I <u>don't appear to have written down</u> his name.*

5 Some verbs are normally used in the passive when they are followed by a 'to'-infinitive clause.

believe	consider	feel	find	know
report	say		think	understand

> *He <u>is said to have died</u> a natural death.*
> *<u>Is</u> it <u>thought to be</u> a good thing?*

Infinitives

6 Some verbs are followed by a 'wh'-word and a 'to'-infinitive clause. These include:

ask	decide	explain	forget
imagine	know	learn	remember
understand	wonder		

> I *didn't know what to call* him.
> She *had forgotten how to ride* a bicycle.

Some verbs are followed by an object, then a 'wh'-word and a 'to'-infinitive clause.

ask	remind	show	teach	tell

> I *asked him what to do.*
> Who will *show him how to use* it?

Some verbs only take 'to'-infinitive clauses to express purpose.
➡ See Unit 97.

> The captain *stopped to reload* the gun.
> He *went to get* some fresh milk.

7 You use a 'to'-infinitive clause after a noun to indicate the aim of an action or the purpose of a physical object.

We arranged a meeting <u>to discuss the new rules.</u>
He had nothing <u>to write with.</u>

You also use a 'to'-infinitive clause after a noun to say that something needs to be done.

I gave him several things <u>to mend.</u>
'What's this?' – 'A list of things <u>to remember.'</u>

8 You use a 'to'-infinitive clause after a noun group that includes an ordinal number, a superlative, or a word like 'next', 'last', or 'only'.

She was the <u>first</u> woman <u>to be elected to the council.</u>
Mr Holmes was <u>the oldest</u> person <u>to be chosen.</u>
The <u>only</u> person <u>to speak</u> was James.

9 You use a 'to'-infinitive clause after abstract nouns to give more specific information about them.

All it takes is <u>a willingness to learn.</u>
He lost <u>the ability to communicate</u> with people.

The following abstract nouns are often followed by a 'to'-infinitive clause:

ability	attempt	chance	desire
failure	inability	need	opportunity
unwillingness	willingness		

Infinitives

Note that the verbs or adjectives which are related to these nouns can also be followed by a 'to'-infinitive clause. For example, you can say 'I attempted to find them', and 'He was willing to learn'.

▶ See Unit 95 for information on nouns that are related to reporting verbs and can be followed by a 'to'-infinitive clause.

Verb + 'to' or '-ing'

Main points

Some verbs take a 'to'-infinitive clause or an '-ing' clause with little difference in meaning. Others take a 'to'-infinitive or '-ing' clause, but the meaning is different.

1 The following verbs can be followed by a 'to'-infinitive clause or an '-ing' clause, with little difference in meaning.

attempt	begin	bother	continue	fear
hate	love	prefer	start	try

> It *started raining*.
> A very cold wind *had started to blow*.
> The captain *didn't bother answering*.
> I *didn't bother to answer*.

Note that if these verbs are used in a continuous tense, they are followed by a 'to'-infinitive clause.

> The company *is beginning to export* to the West.
> We *are continuing to make* good progress.

Verb + 'to' or '-ing'

After 'begin', 'continue', and 'start', you use a 'to'-infinitive clause with the verbs 'understand', 'know', and 'realize'.

>*I <u>began to understand</u> her a bit better.*

2 You can often use 'like' with a 'to'-infinitive or an '-ing' clause with little difference in meaning.

>*I <u>like to fish.</u>*
>*I <u>like fishing.</u>*

However, there is sometimes a difference. You can use 'like' followed by a 'to'-infinitive clause to say that you think something is a good idea, or the right thing to do. You cannot use an '-ing' clause with this meaning.

>*They <u>like to interview</u> you first.*
>*I <u>didn't like to ask</u> him.*

3 After 'remember', 'forget', and 'regret', you use an '-ing' clause if you are referring to an event after it has happened.

>*I <u>remember discussing</u> it once before.*
>*I'll never <u>forget going out</u> with my old aunt.*
>*She did not <u>regret accepting</u> his offer.*

You use a 'to'-infinitive clause after 'remember' and 'forget' if you are referring to an event before it happens.

Verb + 'to' or '-ing'

> *I must <u>remember to send</u> a gift for her child.*
> *Don't <u>forget to send in</u> your entries.*

After 'regret', in formal English, you use a 'to'-infinitive clause with these verbs to say that you are sorry about what you are saying or doing now:

| announce | inform | learn | say | see | tell |

> *I <u>regret to say</u> that it was all burned up.*

4 | If you 'try to do' something, you make an effort to do it. If you 'try doing' something, you do it as an experiment, for example to see if you like it or if it is effective.

> *I <u>tried to explain.</u>*
> *<u>Have</u> you <u>tried painting</u> it?*

5 | If you 'go on doing' something, you continue to do it. If you 'go on to do' something, you do it after you have finished doing something else.

> *I <u>went on writing.</u>*
> *He later <u>went on to form</u> a computer company.*

6 | If you 'are used to doing' something, you are accustomed to doing it. If you 'used to do' something, you did it regularly in the past, but you no longer do it now.

Verb + 'to' or '-ing'

> *We <u>are used to working</u> together.*
> *I <u>used to live</u> in this street.*

7. After 'need', you use a 'to'-infinitive clause if the subject of 'need' is also the subject of the 'to'-infinitive clause. You use an '-ing' form if the subject of 'need' is the object of the '-ing' clause.

> *We <u>need to ask</u> certain questions.*
> *It <u>needs cutting.</u>*

Verbs with other clauses

Main points

'Make' and 'let' can be followed by an object and a base form.

Some verbs of perception can be followed by an object and an '-ing' clause, or an object and a base form.

'Have' and 'get' can be followed by an object and a past participle.

'Dare' is followed by a 'to'-infinitive clause or a base form.

1 You can use an object and a base form after 'make' to say that one person causes another person to do something, or after 'let' to say they allow them to do something.

> *My father <u>made me go</u> for the interview.*
> *Jenny <u>let him talk.</u>*

2 Some verbs of perception are used with an object and an '-ing' clause if an action is unfinished or continues over a period of time, and with an object and a base form if the action is finished.

feel	hear	see	watch

Verbs with other clauses

> He <u>heard a distant voice shouting.</u>
> Dr Hochstadt <u>heard her gasp.</u>

You normally use an '-ing' clause after 'notice', 'observe', 'smell', and 'understand'.

> I could <u>smell Chinese vegetables cooking.</u>
> We can <u>understand them wanting</u> to go.

3 You can use an object and a past participle after 'have' or 'get', when you want to say that someone arranges for something to be done. 'Have' is slightly more formal.

> We'<u>ve</u> just <u>had the house decorated.</u>
> We must <u>get the car repaired.</u>

You also use 'have' and 'get' with an object and a past participle to say that something happens to someone, especially if it is unpleasant.

> She <u>had her purse stolen.</u>
> He <u>got his car broken into</u> at the weekend.

4 You use 'have' followed by an object and an '-ing' clause, or an object and a past participle, when you want to say that someone causes something to happen, either intentionally or unintentionally.

> Alan <u>had me looking</u> for that book all day.
> He <u>had me</u> utterly <u>confused.</u>

5 You use 'want' and 'would like' with an object and a past participle to indicate that you want something to be done.

> I _want the work finished_ by January 1st.
> How _would_ you _like your hair cut,_ sir?

6 'Dare' can be followed by a 'to'-infinitive clause or a base form in negative or interrogative sentences:

● when there is an auxiliary or modal before 'dare'

> He _did_ not _dare to walk_ to the village.
> What bank _would dare offer_ such terms?

● when you use the form 'dares' or 'dared' (but not 'dares not' or 'dared not')

> No one _dares disturb_ him.
> No other manager _dared to compete._

You must use a base form in:

● negative or interrogative sentences without an auxiliary or modal before 'dare'

> I _daren't ring_ Jeremy again.
> Nobody _dare disturb_ him.
> _Dare_ she _go in?_

● negative sentences with 'dares not' or 'dared not'

> He _dares not risk_ it.
> Sonny _dared not disobey._

Verbs with other clauses

Note that the phrase 'how dare you' is always followed by a base form.

How <u>dare</u> you <u>speak</u> to me like that?

'Dare' is rarely used in affirmative sentences.

Link verbs

Main points

Link verbs are used to join the subject with a complement.

Link verbs can have adjectives, noun groups, or 'to'-infinitive clauses as complements.

You can use 'it' and 'there' as impersonal subjects with link verbs.

1 A small but important group of verbs are followed by a complement rather than an object. The complement tells you more about the subject. Verbs that take complements are called 'link' verbs.

appear	be	become	feel
get	go	grow	keep
look	prove	remain	seem
smell	sound	stay	taste
turn			

> I *am* proud of these people.
> She *was getting* too old to play tennis.
> They *looked* all right to me.

Link verbs

2 Link verbs often have adjectives as complements describing the subject.

> *We <u>felt</u> very happy.*
> *He <u>was</u> the tallest in the room.*

➤ See Units 31 to 33 and Unit 47 for more information about adjectives after link verbs.

3 You can use link verbs with noun groups as complements to give your opinion about the subject.

> *He's not <u>the right man for it.</u>*
> *She seemed <u>an ideal person to look after them.</u>*

You also use noun groups as complements after 'be', 'become', and 'remain' to specify the subject.

> *He became <u>a geologist.</u>*
> *Promises by MPs remained just <u>promises.</u>*
> *This one is <u>yours.</u>*

Note that you use object pronouns after 'be'.

> *It's <u>me</u> again.*

4 Some link verbs can have 'to'-infinitive clauses as complements.

| appear | get | grow | look | prove | seem |

Link verbs

He appears <u>to have taken my keys.</u>
She seemed <u>to like me.</u>

These verbs, and 'remain', can also be followed by 'to be' and a complement.

Mary <u>seemed to be</u> asleep.
His new job <u>proved to be</u> a challenge.

5 You can use 'it' and 'there' as impersonal subjects with link verbs.

It <u>seems</u> silly not to tell him.
There <u>appears</u> to have been a terrible mistake.

► See Units 17 and 18 for more information.

You can use 'be' with some abstract nouns as the subject, followed by a 'that'-clause or a 'to'-infinitive clause as the complement.

| advice | agreement | answer | decision |
| idea | plan | problem | solution |

<u>The answer is</u> that they are simply not interested in it.
<u>The idea was</u> to spend more money on basic training.

Link verbs

Some can only have a 'that'-clause.

| conclusion explanation fact feeling |
| reason report thought understanding |

The fact is that I can't go to the party.

Reporting the past

Main points

A report structure is used to report what people say or think.

You use the present tense of the reporting verb when you are reporting something that someone says or thinks at the time you are speaking.

You often use past tenses in report structures because a reported clause usually reports something that was said or believed in the past.

1. You use a report structure to report what people say or think. A report structure consists of two parts. One part is the reporting clause, which contains the reporting verb.

> *I told him nothing was going to happen to me.*
> *I agreed that he should do it.*

The other part is the reported clause.

> *He felt that he had to do something.*
> *Henry said he wanted to go home.*

Reporting the past

▶ See Units 75-77 for more information on report structures.

2 For the verb in the reporting clause, you choose a tense that is appropriate at the time you are speaking.

Because reports are usually about something that was said or believed in the past, both the reporting verb and the verb in the reported clause are often in a past tense.

> *Mrs Kaur <u>announced</u> that the lecture <u>had begun.</u>*
> *At the time we <u>thought</u> that he <u>was</u> mad.*

3 Although you normally use past tenses in reports about the past, you can use a present tense in the reported clause if what you are saying is important in the present, for example:

● because you want to emphasize that it is still true

> *<u>Did</u> you <u>tell</u> him that this young woman <u>is looking</u> for a job?*

● because you want to give advice or a warning, or make a suggestion for the present or future

> *I <u>told</u> you they <u>have</u> this class on Friday afternoon, so you should have come a bit earlier.*

4 You use a present tense for the reporting verb when you are reporting:

● what someone says or thinks at the time you are speaking

> She <u>says</u> she wants to see you this afternoon.
> I <u>think</u> there's something wrong.

Note that, as in the last example, it may be your own thoughts that you are reporting.

● what someone often says

> He <u>says</u> that no one understands him.

● what someone has said in the past, if what they said is still true

> My doctor <u>says</u> it's nothing to worry about.

5 If you are predicting what people will say or think, you use a future tense for the reporting verb.

> No doubt he <u>will claim</u> that his car broke down.
> They <u>will think</u> we are making a fuss.

6 You very rarely try to report the exact words of a statement. You usually give a summary of what was said. For example, John might say:

'I tried to phone you about six times yesterday. I let the phone ring for ages but there was no answer. I couldn't get through at all so I finally gave up.'

Reporting the past

You would probably report this as:
John said he tried to phone several times yesterday, but he couldn't get through.

7 When you are telling a story of your own, or one that you have heard from someone else, direct speech simply becomes part of the narrative.
In this extract a taxi driver picks up a passenger:

> *'What part of London are you headed for?' I asked him.*
> *'I'm going to Epsom for the races. It's Derby day today.'*
> *'So it is,' I said. 'I wish I were going with you. I love betting on horses.'*

You might report this as part of the narrative without reporting verbs:

My passenger was going to Epsom to see the Derby, and I wanted to go with him.

Reported questions

Main points

You use reported questions to talk about a question that someone else has asked.

In reported questions, the subject of the question comes before the verb.

You use 'if' or 'whether' in reported 'yes/no'-questions.

1. When you are talking about a question that someone has asked, you use a reported question.

> *She asked me <u>why I was so late.</u>*
> *He wanted to know <u>where I was going.</u>*
> *I demanded to know <u>what was going on.</u>*
> *I asked her <u>if I could help her.</u>*
> *I asked her <u>whether there was anything wrong.</u>*

In formal and written English, 'enquire' (also spelled 'inquire') is often used instead of 'ask'.

> *Wilkie had enquired <u>if she did a lot of acting.</u>*
> *He inquired <u>whether he could see her.</u>*

Reported questions

2 When you are reporting a question, the verb in the reported clause is often in a past tense. This is because you are often talking about the past when you are reporting someone else's words.

> *She <u>asked</u> me why I <u>was</u> so late.*
> *Pat <u>asked</u> him if she <u>had hurt</u> him.*

However, you can use a present or future tense if the question you are reporting relates to the present or future.

> *Mark <u>was asking</u> if you<u>'re enjoying</u> your new job.*
> *They <u>asked</u> if you<u>'ll be</u> there tomorrow night.*

3 In reported questions, the subject of the question comes before the verb, just as it does in affirmative sentences.

> *She asked me why <u>I was late.</u>*
> *I asked what <u>he was doing.</u>*

4 You do not normally use the auxiliary 'do' in reported questions.

> *She asked him if <u>his parents spoke</u> French or German.*
> *They asked us what <u>we thought.</u>*

Reported questions

The auxiliary 'do' can be used in reported questions, but only for emphasis, or to make a contrast with something that has already been said. It is not put before the subject as in direct questions.

> *She asked me whether I really <u>did</u> mean what I'd said.*
> *I told him I didn't like classical music. He asked me what kind of music I <u>did</u> like.*

5 You use 'if' or 'whether' to introduce reported 'yes/no'-questions.

> *I asked him <u>if</u> he was on holiday.*
> *The bride's mother asked me <u>if</u> anything was wrong.*
> *She hugged him and asked him <u>whether</u> he was all right.*
> *I asked him <u>whether</u> he was single.*

'Whether' is used especially when there is a choice of possibilities.

> *I was asked <u>whether</u> I wanted to stay at a hotel <u>or</u> at his home.*
> *They asked <u>whether</u> Tim was <u>or</u> was <u>not</u> in the team.*
> *I asked him <u>whether</u> he loved me <u>or</u> not.*

Reported questions

Note that you can put 'or not' immediately after 'whether', but not immediately after 'if'.

The police didn't ask <u>whether or not</u> they were in.

➤ See Units 74, 76, and 77 for more information on reporting.

Reporting: 'that'-clauses

Main points

You usually use your own words to report what someone said, rather than repeating their exact words.

Report structures contain a reporting clause first, then a reported clause.

When you are reporting a statement, the reported clause is a 'that'-clause.

You must mention the hearer with 'tell'. You need not mention the hearer with 'say'.

1 When you are reporting what someone said, you do not usually repeat their exact words, you use your own words in a report structure.

Jim said he wanted to go home.

Jim's actual words might have been 'It's time I went' or 'I must go'.

Report structures contain two clauses. The first clause is the reporting clause, which contains a reporting verb such as 'say', 'tell', or 'ask'.

Reporting: 'that'-clauses

> *She said* that she'd been to Belgium.
> *The man in the shop told me* how much it
> would cost.

You often use verbs that refer to people's thoughts
and feelings to report what people say. If someone
says 'I am wrong', you might report this as 'He **felt**
that he was wrong'. ➤ See Unit 77.

2 The second clause in a report structure is the
reported clause, which contains the information
that you are reporting. The reported clause can be
a 'that'-clause, a 'to'-infinitive clause, an 'if'-clause,
or a 'wh'-word clause.

> *She said <u>that she didn't know.</u>*
> *He told me <u>to do it.</u>*
> *Mary asked <u>if she could stay with us.</u>*
> *She asked <u>where he'd gone.</u>*

3 If you want to report a statement, you use a 'that'-
clause after a verb such as 'say'.

admit	agree	answer	argue
claim	complain	decide	deny
explain	insist	mention	promise
reply	say	warn	

> *He <u>said that</u> he would go.*
> *I <u>replied that</u> I had not read it yet.*

Reporting: 'that'-clauses

You often omit 'that' from the 'that'-clause, but not after 'answer', 'argue', 'explain', or 'reply'.

> *They <u>said</u> I had to see a doctor first.*
> *He <u>answered that</u> the price would be three pounds.*

You often mention the hearer after the preposition 'to' with the following verbs.

admit	announce	complain	explain
mention	say	suggest	

> *He <u>complained to me</u> that you were rude.*

4 'Tell' and some other reporting verbs are also used with a 'that'-clause, but with these verbs you have to mention the hearer as the object of the verb.

convince	inform	notify	persuade
reassure	remind	tell	

> *He <u>told me</u> that he was a farmer.*
> *I <u>informed her</u> that I could not come.*

The word 'that' is often omitted after 'tell'.

> *I <u>told them</u> you were at the dentist.*

You can also mention the hearer as the object of the verb with 'promise' and 'warn'.

> *I <u>promised her</u> that I wouldn't be late.*

Reporting: 'that'-clauses

5 Note the differences between 'say' and 'tell'. You cannot use 'say' with the hearer as the object of the verb. You cannot say 'I said them you had gone'. You cannot use 'tell' without the hearer as the object of the verb. You cannot say 'I told that you had gone'. You cannot use 'tell' with 'to' and the hearer. You cannot say 'I told to them you had gone'.

6 The reporting verbs that have the hearer as object, such as 'tell', can be used in the passive.

> *She <u>was told</u> that there were no tickets left.*

Most reporting verbs that do not need the hearer as object, such as 'say', can be used in the passive with impersonal 'it' as subject, but not 'answer', 'complain', 'insist', 'promise', 'reply', or 'warn'.

> *<u>It was said</u> that the money had been stolen.*

➤ See also Units 74 and 77.

Main points

When reporting an order, a request, or a piece of advice, the reported clause is a 'to'-infinitive clause, used after an object.

When reporting a question, the reported clause is an 'if'-clause or a 'wh'-word clause.

Many reporting verbs refer to people's thoughts and feelings.

1 If you want to report an order, a request, or a piece of advice, you use a 'to'-infinitive clause after a reporting verb such as 'tell', 'ask', or 'advise'. You mention the hearer as the object of the verb, before the 'to'-infinitive clause.

advise	ask	beg	command
forbid	instruct	invite	order
persuade	remind	tell	warn

> Johnson <u>told her to wake</u> him <u>up.</u>
> He <u>ordered me to fetch</u> the books.
> He <u>asked her to marry</u> him.
> He <u>advised me to buy</u> it.

Other report structures

If the order, request, or advice is negative, you put 'not' before the 'to'-infinitive.

> *He had ordered his officers <u>not to use</u> any weapons.*
> *She asked her staff <u>not to discuss</u> it publicly.*
> *Doctors advised him <u>not to play</u> for three weeks.*

If the subject of the 'to'-infinitive clause is the same as the subject of the main verb, you can use 'ask' or 'beg' to report a request without mentioning the hearer.

> *I <u>asked to see</u> the manager.*
> *Both men <u>begged not to be named.</u>*

2 If you want to report a question, you use a verb such as 'ask' followed by an 'if'-clause or a 'wh'-word clause.

> *I <u>asked if</u> I could stay with them.*
> *They <u>wondered whether</u> the time was right.*
> *He <u>asked</u> me <u>where</u> I was going.*
> *She <u>inquired how</u> Ibrahim was getting on.*

Note that in reported questions, the subject of the question comes before the verb, just as it does in affirmative sentences.
➤ See Unit 75.

Other report structures

3 Many reporting verbs refer to people's thoughts and feelings but are often used to report what people say. For example, if someone says 'I must go', you might report this as 'She wanted to go' or 'She thought she should go'.

Some of these verbs are followed by:

● a 'that'-clause

accept	believe	consider	fear
feel	guess	imagine	know
suppose	think	understand	worry

> We both <u>knew</u> that the town was cut off.
> I had always <u>believed</u> that I would see him again.

● a 'to'-infinitive clause

intend	plan	want

> He doesn't <u>want</u> to get up.

● a 'that'-clause or a 'to'-infinitive clause

agree	decide	expect	forget	hope
prefer	regret	remember	wish	

> She <u>hoped she wasn't going to cry.</u>
> They are in love and <u>wish to marry.</u>

Other report structures

'Expect' and 'prefer' can also be followed by an object and a 'to'-infinitive.

> *I'm sure she <u>doesn't expect you to take</u> the plane.*
> *The headmaster <u>prefers them to act</u> plays they have written themselves.*

4 A speaker's exact words are more often used in stories than in ordinary conversation.

> *'I knew I'd seen you,' I said.*
> *'Only one,' replied the Englishman.*
> *'Let's go and have a look at the swimming pool,' she suggested.*

The passive voice

Main points

You use the passive voice to focus on the person or thing affected by an action.

You form the passive by using a form of 'be' and a past participle.

Only verbs that have an object can have a passive form. With verbs that can have two objects, either object can be the subject of the passive.

1 When you want to talk about the person or thing that performs an action, you use the active voice.

> *Mr Smith <u>locks</u> the gate at 6 o'clock every night.*
> *The storm <u>destroyed</u> dozens of trees.*

When you want to focus on the person or thing that is affected by an action, rather than the person or thing that performs the action, you use the passive voice.

> *The gate <u>is locked</u> at 6 o'clock every night.*
> *Dozens of trees <u>were destroyed.</u>*

2 The passive is formed with a form of the auxiliary 'be', followed by the past participle of a main verb.

The passive voice

Two new stores <u>were opened</u> this year.
The room <u>had been cleaned.</u>

Continuous passive tenses are formed with a form of the auxiliary 'be' followed by 'being' and the past participle of a main verb.

Jobs <u>are</u> still <u>being lost.</u>
It <u>was being done</u> without his knowledge.

3 After modals you use the base form 'be' followed by the past participle of a main verb.

What <u>can be done</u>?
We <u>won't be beaten.</u>

When you are talking about the past, you use a modal with 'have been' followed by the past participle of a main verb.

He <u>may have been given</u> the car.
He <u>couldn't have been told</u> by Jimmy.

4 You form passive infinitives by using 'to be' or 'to have been' followed by the past participle of a main verb.

He wanted <u>to be forgiven.</u>
The car was reported <u>to have been stolen.</u>

5 In informal English, 'get' is sometimes used instead of 'be' to form the passive.

The passive voice

> *Our car <u>gets cleaned</u> every weekend.*
> *He <u>got killed</u> in a plane crash.*

6 When you use the passive, you often do not mention the person or thing that performs the action at all. This may be because you do not know or do not want to say who it is, or because it does not matter.

> *Her boyfriend <u>was shot</u> in the chest.*
> *Your application <u>was rejected.</u>*
> *Such items should <u>be</u> carefully <u>packed</u> in tea chests.*

7 If you are using the passive and you do want to mention the person or thing that performs the action, you use 'by'.

> *He had been poisoned <u>by</u> his girlfriend.*
> *He was brought up <u>by</u> an aunt.*

You use 'with' to talk about something that is used to perform the action.

> *A circle was drawn in the dirt <u>with</u> a stick.*
> *He was killed <u>with</u> a knife.*

8 Only verbs that usually have an object can have a passive form. You can say 'people spend money' or 'money is spent'.

The passive voice

An enormous amount of money <u>is spent</u> on beer.
The food <u>is sold</u> at local markets.

With verbs which can have two objects, you can form two different passive sentences. For example, you can say 'The secretary was given the key' or 'The key was given to the secretary'.

They <u>were offered</u> a new flat.
The books <u>will be sent</u> to you.

➤ See Unit 52 for more information on verbs that can have two objects.

Main points

The modal verbs are: 'can', 'could', 'may', 'might', 'must', 'ought', 'shall', 'should', 'will', and 'would'.

Modals are always the first word in a verb group.

All modals except for 'ought' are followed by the base form of a verb.

'Ought' is followed by a 'to'-infinitive.

Modals have only one form.

Modals can be used for various different purposes. These are explained in Units 80–91.

1 Modals are always the first word in a verb group. All modals except for 'ought' are followed by the base form of a verb.

> I _must leave_ fairly soon.
> I think it _will look_ rather nice.
> Things _might have been_ so different.
> People _may be watching._

Introduction to modals

2 'Ought' is always followed by a 'to'-infinitive.

> *She <u>ought to go</u> straight back to New Zealand.*
> *Sam <u>ought to have realized</u> how dangerous it was.*
> *You <u>ought to be doing</u> this.*

3 Modals have only one form. There is no '-s' form for the third person singular of the present tense, and there are no '-ing' or '-ed' forms.

> *There's nothing <u>I can</u> do about it.*
> *I'm sure <u>he can</u> do it.*
> *<u>You must</u> see the painting he has given me.*

4 Modals do not normally indicate the time when something happens. There are, however, a few exceptions.

'Shall' and 'will' often indicate a future event or situation.

> *I <u>shall</u> do what you suggested.*
> *He <u>will</u> not return for many hours.*

'Could' is used as the past form of 'can' to express ability. 'Would' is used as the past form of 'will' to express the future.

When I was young, I <u>could</u> run for miles and miles.
He remembered that he <u>would</u> see his mother the next day.

5 In spoken English and informal written English, 'shall' and 'will' are shortened to '-'ll', and 'would' to '-'d', and added to a pronoun.

<u>I'll</u> see you tomorrow.
I hope <u>you'll</u> agree.
Posy said <u>she'd</u> love to stay.

'Shall', 'will', and 'would' are never shortened if they come at the end of a sentence.

Paul promised that he would come, and I hope he <u>will.</u>
I'm doing exactly what I said I <u>would.</u>

In spoken English, you can also add '-'ll' and '-'d' to nouns.

My <u>car'll</u> be outside.
The <u>headmaster'd</u> be furious if he found out about it.

Introduction to modals

⊖ WARNING: Remember that '-d' is also the short form of the auxiliary 'had'.

I'<u>d</u> heard it many times.

Main points

You use negative words with modals to make negative clauses.

Modals go in front of the subject in questions.

You never use two modals together.

1. To make a clause negative, you put a negative word immediately after the modal.

> You <u>must not</u> worry.
> I <u>can never</u> remember his name.
> He <u>ought not</u> to have done that.

'Can not' is always written as one word, 'cannot'.

> I <u>cannot</u> go back.

However, if 'can' is followed by 'not only', 'can' and 'not' are not joined.

> We <u>can not only</u> book your flight for you, but also advise you about hotels.

2. In spoken English and informal written English, 'not' is often shortened to '-n't' and added to the

modal. The following modals are often shortened in this way:

could not:	couldn't
should not:	shouldn't
must not:	mustn't
would not:	wouldn't

> *We <u>couldn't</u> leave the farm.*
> *You <u>mustn't</u> talk about Ron like that.*
> *I <u>shouldn't</u> have said what I did.*

Note the following irregular short forms:

shall not:	shan't
will not:	won't
cannot:	can't

> *I <u>shan't</u> let you go.*
> *<u>Won't</u> you change your mind?*
> *We <u>can't</u> stop now.*

'Might not' and 'ought not' are sometimes shortened to 'mightn't' and 'oughtn't'.

> *He <u>mightn't</u> be back until tonight.*
> *Perhaps I <u>oughtn't</u> to interfere.*

Note that 'may not' is very rarely shortened to 'mayn't' in modern English.

3 To make a question, you put the modal in front of the subject.

> _Could you_ give me an example?
> _Will you_ be coming in later?
> _Shall I_ shut the door?

Modals are also used in question tags.

▶ See Units 7 and 8 for more information.

4 You never use two modals together. For example, you cannot say 'He will can come'. Instead you can say 'He will be able to come'.

> I _shall have to_ go.
> Your husband _might have to_ give up work.

5 Instead of using modals, you can often use other verbs and expressions to make requests, offers, or suggestions, to express wishes or intentions, or to show that you are being polite.

For example, 'be able to' is used instead of 'can', 'be likely to' is used instead of 'might', and 'have to' is used instead of 'must'.

> All members _are able to_ claim expenses.
> I think that we _are likely to_ see more of this.

Modals – negation, questions

These expressions are also used after modals.

> *I really thought I <u>wouldn't be able to</u> visit you this week.*

6 'Dare' and 'need' sometimes behave like modals.

➤ See Unit 72 for information on 'dare' and Units 71 and 90 for information on 'need'.

Possibility

Main points

You use 'can' to say that something is possible.

You use 'could', 'might', and 'may' to indicate that you are not certain whether something is possible, but you think it is.

1. When you want to say that something is possible, you use 'can'.

> Cooking _can_ be a real pleasure.
> In some cases this _can_ cause difficulty.

You use 'cannot' or 'can't' to say that something is not possible.

> This _cannot_ be the answer.
> You _can't_ be serious.

2. When you want to indicate that you are not certain whether something is possible, but you think it is, you use 'could', 'might', or 'may'. There is no important difference in meaning between these modals, but 'may' is slightly more formal.

> That _could_ be one reason.
> He _might_ come.
> They _may_ help us.

Possibility

You can also use 'might not' or 'may not' in this way.

> *He <u>might not</u> be in England at all.*
> *They <u>may not</u> get a house with central heating.*

Note that 'could not' normally refers to ability in the past. ➤ See Unit 83.

3 | When there is a possibility that something happened in the past, but you are not certain if it actually happened, you use 'could have', 'may have', or 'might have', followed by a past participle.

> *It <u>could have been</u> tomato soup.*
> *You <u>may have noticed</u> this advertisement.*

You can also use 'might not have' or 'may not have' in this way.

> *He <u>might not have seen</u> me.*
> *They <u>may not have done</u> it.*

You use 'could not have' when you want to indicate that it is not possible that something happened.

> *He didn't have a boat, so he <u>couldn't have rowed</u> away.*
> *It <u>couldn't have been</u> wrong.*

You also use 'could have' to say that there was a possibility of something happening in the past, but it did not happen.

It <u>could have been</u> awful. (But it wasn't awful.)
You <u>could have got</u> a job last year. (But you
didn't get a job.)

4 You also use 'might have' or 'could have' followed
by a past participle to say that if a particular thing
had happened, then there was a possibility of
something else happening.

*She said it <u>might have been</u> all right, if the
weather had been good.* (But the weather
wasn't good, so it wasn't all right.)
If I'd been there, I <u>could have helped</u> you. (But I
wasn't there, so I couldn't help you.)

5 'Be able to', 'not be able to', and 'be unable to' are
sometimes used instead of 'can' and 'cannot', for
example after another modal, or when you want
to use a 'to'-infinitive, an '-ing' form, or a past participle.

When <u>will I be able to</u> pick them up?
He had <u>been unable to</u> get a ticket.

6 You use 'used to be able to' to say that something
was possible in the past, but is not possible now.

Everyone <u>used to be able to</u> have free eye tests.
*You <u>used to be able to</u> buy cigarettes in packs of
five.*

Possibility

7 Note that you also use 'could' followed by a negative word and the comparative form of an adjective to emphasize a quality that someone or something has. For example, if you say 'I couldn't be happier', you mean that you are very happy indeed and cannot imagine being happier than you are now.

> You _couldn't_ be _more wrong._
> He _could hardly_ have felt _more ashamed_ of himself.

Main points

You use 'must', 'ought', 'should', or 'will' to express probability or certainty.

You use 'cannot' or 'can't' as the negative of 'must', rather than 'must not' or 'mustn't', to say that something is not probable or is not certain.

1. When you want to say that something is probably true or that it will probably happen, you use 'should' or 'ought'. 'Should' is followed by the base form of a verb. 'Ought' is followed by a 'to'-infinitive.

> We _should_ arrive by dinner time.
> She _ought_ to know.

When you want to say that you think something is probably not true or that it will probably not happen, you use 'should not' or 'ought not'.

> There _shouldn't_ be any problem.
> That _ought not_ to be too difficult.

2. When you want to say that you are fairly sure that something has happened, you use 'should have' or

Probability and certainty

'ought to have', followed by a past participle.

> *You <u>should have</u> heard by now that I'm O.K.*
> *They <u>ought to have</u> arrived yesterday.*

When you want to say that you do not think that something has happened, you use 'should not have' or 'ought not to have', followed by a past participle.

> *You <u>shouldn't have</u> had any difficulty in getting there.*
> *This <u>ought not to have</u> been a problem.*

3 You also use 'should have' or 'ought to have' to say that you expected something to happen, but that it did not happen.

> *Yesterday <u>should have been</u> the start of the soccer season.*
> *She <u>ought to have been</u> home by now.*

Note that you do not normally use the negative forms with this meaning.

4 When you are fairly sure that something is the case, you use 'must'.

> *Oh, you <u>must</u> be Sylvia's husband.*
> *He <u>must</u> know something about it.*

If you are fairly sure that something is not the case, you use 'cannot' or 'can't'.

> *This <u>cannot</u> be the whole story.*
> *He <u>can't</u> be very old – he's about 25, isn't he?*

⊖ WARNING: You do not use 'must not' or 'mustn't' with this meaning.

5 When you want to say that you are almost certain that something has happened, you use 'must have', followed by a past participle.

> *This article <u>must have been</u> written by a woman.*
> *We <u>must have taken</u> the wrong road.*

To say that you do not think that something has happened, you use 'can't have', followed by a past participle.

> *You <u>can't have forgotten</u> me.*
> *He <u>can't have said</u> that.*

6 You use 'will' or '-'ll' to say that something is certain to happen in the future.

> *People <u>will</u> always say things you want to hear.*
> *They'<u>ll</u> manage.*

You use 'will not' or 'won't' to say that something is certain not to happen.

> *You <u>won't</u> get much sympathy from them.*

Probability and certainty

7 There are several ways of talking about probability and certainty without using modals. For example, you can use:

● 'bound to' followed by the base form of a verb

> *It was <u>bound to</u> happen.*
> *You're <u>bound to</u> make a mistake.*

● an adjective such as 'certain', 'likely', 'sure', or 'unlikely', followed by a 'to'-infinitive clause or a 'that'-clause

> *They were <u>certain</u> that you were defeated.*
> *I am not <u>likely</u> to forget it.*

➤ See Unit 33 for more information on these adjectives.

Main points

You use 'can' to talk about ability in the present and in the future.

You use 'could' to talk about ability in the past.

You use 'be able to' to talk about ability in the present, future, and past.

1 You use 'can' to say that someone has the ability to do something.

> *You can all read and write.*
> *Anybody can become a qualified teacher.*

You use 'cannot' or 'can't' to say that they do not have the ability to do something.

> *He cannot dance.*
> *I can't speak German.*

2 When you want to talk about someone's ability in the past as a result of a skill they had or did not have, you use 'could', 'could not', or 'couldn't'.

> *He could run faster than anyone else.*
> *A lot of them couldn't read or write.*

Ability

3 You also use 'be able to', 'not be able to', and 'be unable to' to talk about someone's ability to do something, but 'can' and 'could' are more common.

> *She <u>was able to</u> tie her own shoelaces.*
> *They <u>are not able to</u> run very fast.*
> *Many people <u>were unable to</u> read or write.*

4 You use 'was able to' and 'were able to' to say that someone managed to do something in a particular situation in the past.

> *After treatment he <u>was able to</u> return to work.*
> *The farmers <u>were able to</u> pay the new wages.*
> *We <u>were able to</u> find time to discuss it.*

⊖ WARNING: You do not normally use 'could' to say that someone managed to do something in a particular situation. However, you can use 'could not' or 'couldn't' to say that someone did not manage to do something in a particular situation.

> *We <u>couldn't</u> stop laughing.*
> *I just <u>couldn't</u> think of anything to say.*

5 When you want to say that someone had the ability to do something in the past, but did not do it, you use 'could have' followed by a past participle.

You <u>could have given</u> it all to me.
You know, she <u>could have done</u> French.

You often use this form when you want to express disapproval about something that was not done.

You <u>could have been</u> a little bit tidier.
You <u>could have told</u> me!

6 You use 'could not have' or 'couldn't have' followed by a past participle to say that it is not possible that someone had the ability to do something.

I <u>couldn't have gone</u> with you, because I was in London at the time.
She <u>couldn't have taken</u> the car, because Jim was using it.

7 In most cases, you can choose to use 'can' or 'be able to'. However, you sometimes have to use 'be able to'. You have to use 'be able to' if you are using another modal, or if you want to use an '-ing' form, a past participle, or a 'to'-infinitive.

Nobody else <u>will be able to</u> read it.
…the satisfaction of <u>being able to</u> do the job.
I don't think I'd have <u>been able to</u> get an answer.
You're foolish to expect <u>to be able to</u> do that.

Ability

8 You also use 'can' or 'could' with verbs such as 'see', 'hear', and 'smell' to say that someone is or was aware of something through one of their senses.

> *I <u>can smell</u> gas.*
> *I <u>can't see</u> her.*
> *I <u>could see</u> a few stars in the sky.*
> *There was such a noise we <u>couldn't hear.</u>*

Main points

You use 'can' or 'be allowed to' to talk about whether someone has permission to do something or not.

You usually use 'can' to give someone permission to do something.

You usually use 'can' or 'could' to ask for permission to do something.

1 You use 'can' to say that someone is allowed to do something. You use 'cannot' or 'can't' to say that they are not allowed to do it.

> *Students <u>can</u> take a year away from university.*
> *Children <u>cannot</u> bathe except in the presence of two lifesavers.*

You use 'could' to say that someone was allowed to do something in the past. You use 'could not' or 'couldn't' to say that they were not allowed to do it.

> *They <u>could</u> go to any part of the island they wanted.*

Permission

> *Both students and staff <u>could</u> use the swimming pool.*
> *We <u>couldn't</u> go into the library after 5 pm.*

2. You also use 'be allowed to' when you are talking about permission, but not when you are asking for it or giving it.

> *When Mr Wilt asks for a solicitor he will <u>be allowed to</u> see one.*
> *It was only after several months that I <u>was allowed to</u> visit her.*
> *You<u>'re</u> not <u>allowed to</u> use calculators in exams.*

3. In more formal situations, 'may' is used to say that someone is allowed to do something, and 'may not' is used to say that they are not allowed to do it.

> *They <u>may</u> do exactly as they like.*
> *The retailer <u>may not</u> sell that book below the publisher's price.*

4. When you want to give someone permission to do something, you use 'can'.

> *You <u>can</u> borrow that pen if you want to.*
> *You <u>can</u> go off duty now.*
> *She <u>can</u> go with you.*

'May' is also used to give permission, but this is more formal.

You <u>may</u> speak.
You <u>may</u> leave as soon as you have finished.

5 When you want to refuse someone permission to do something, you use 'cannot', 'can't', 'will not', 'won't', 'shall not', or 'shan't'.

'Can I have some sweets?' – 'No, you <u>can't!</u>'
'I'll just go upstairs.' – 'You <u>will not!</u>'
You <u>shan't</u> leave without my permission.

6 When you are asking for permission to do something, you use 'can' or 'could'. If you ask in a very simple and direct way, you use 'can'.

<u>Can</u> I ask a question?
<u>Can</u> we have something to wipe our hands on please?

'Could' is more polite than 'can'.

<u>Could</u> I just interrupt a minute?
<u>Could</u> we put this fire on?

'May' is also used to ask permission, but this is more formal.

<u>May</u> I have a cigarette?

'Might' is rather old-fashioned and is not often used in modern English in this way.

<u>Might</u> I inquire if you are the owner?

Permission

7 You have to use 'be allowed to' instead of a modal if you are using another modal, or if you want to use an '-ing' form, a past participle, or a 'to'-infinitive.

> Teachers <u>will be allowed to</u> decide for themselves.
>
> I am strongly in favour of people <u>being allowed to</u> put on plays.
>
> They have not <u>been allowed to</u> come.
>
> We were going <u>to be allowed to</u> travel on the trains.

Instructions and requests

Main points

You use 'Could you' to tell someone politely to do something.

Imperatives are not very polite.

You also use 'Could you' to ask someone politely for help.

You use 'I would like', 'Would you mind', 'Do you think you could', and 'I wonder if you could' to make requests.

1 When you want to tell someone to do something, you can use 'Could you', 'Will you', and 'Would you'. 'Could you' is very polite.

> _Could you_ make out her bill, please?
> _Could you_ just switch on the light behind you?

'Will you' and 'Would you' are normally used by people in authority. 'Would you' is more polite than 'Will you'.

> _Would you_ tell her that Adrian phoned?
> _Will you_ please leave the room?

Instructions and requests

Note that although these sentences look like questions ('Will you', not 'You will'), they are not really questions.

2 | If someone in authority wants to tell someone to do something, they sometimes say 'I would like you to do this' or 'I'd like you to do this'.

> *Penelope, I <u>would like</u> you to get us the files.*
> *I'<u>d like</u> you to finish this work by Thursday.*

3 | You can use an imperative to tell someone to do something, but this is not very polite.

> <u>*Stop*</u> *her.*
> <u>*Go*</u> *away, all of you.*

However, imperatives are commonly used when talking to people you know very well.

> <u>*Come*</u> *here, love.*
> <u>*Sit down*</u> *and let me get you a drink.*

You often use imperatives in situations of danger or urgency.

> <u>*Look out!*</u> *There's a car coming.*
> <u>*Put*</u> *it <u>away</u> before Mum sees you.*

4 | When you want to ask someone to help you, you use 'Could you', 'Would you', 'Can you', or 'Will you'. 'Could you' and 'Would you' are used in formal situations, or when you want to be very polite,

for example because you are asking for something that requires a lot of effort. 'Could you' is more polite than 'Would you'.

> <u>Could you</u> show me how to do this?
> <u>Would you</u> do me a favour?

'Will you' and 'Can you' are used in informal situations, especially when you are not asking for something that requires a lot of effort.

> <u>Will you</u> post this for me on your way to work?
> <u>Can you</u> make me a copy of that?

5 You also use 'I would like' or 'I'd like', followed by a 'to'-infinitive or a noun group, to make a request.

> <u>I would like</u> to ask you one question.
> <u>I'd like</u> steak and chips, please.

6 You can also make a request by using:

- 'Would you mind', followed by an '-ing' form

> <u>Would you mind</u> doing the washing up?
> <u>Would you mind</u> waiting a moment?

- 'Do you think you could', followed by the base form of a verb

> <u>Do you think you could</u> help me?

Instructions and requests

● 'I wonder if you could', followed by the base form of a verb

> *I wonder if you could* *look after my cat for me while I'm away?*

Suggestions

Main points

You use 'could', 'couldn't', or 'shall' to make a suggestion.

You use 'Shall we' to suggest doing something with someone.

You use 'You might like' or 'You might want' to make polite suggestions.

You use 'may as well' or 'might as well' to suggest a sensible action.

You use 'What about', 'Let's', 'Why don't', and 'Why not' to make suggestions.

1 You use 'could' to suggest doing something.

> *You <u>could</u> phone her.*
> *She <u>could</u> go into research.*
> *We <u>could</u> go to the cinema on Friday after work.*

You also use 'couldn't' in a question to suggest doing something.

Suggestions

> *Couldn't you just build some more new factories?*
> *Couldn't we do it at the weekend?*
> *Couldn't I just lie down in the cabin?*

2. You use 'Shall we' to suggest doing something with somebody else.

> *Shall we go and see a film?*
> *Shall we talk about something different now?*

You use 'Shall I' to suggest doing something yourself.

> *Shall I contact the Chairman?*

3. You use 'You might', followed by a verb meaning 'like' or 'want', to make a suggestion in a very polite way.

> *I thought perhaps you might like to come along with me.*
> *You might want to try another shop.*

You can also do this using 'It might be', followed by a noun group or an adjective, and a 'to'-infinitive.

> *I think it might be a good idea to stop recording now.*
> *It might be wise to get a new car.*

4. You use 'may as well' or 'might as well' to suggest doing something, but only because it seems the sensible thing to do, or because there is no reason not to do it.

> You <u>may as well</u> open them all.
> He <u>might as well</u> take the car.

5. You can also make a suggestion by using:

● 'What about' or 'How about' followed by an '-ing' form

> <u>What about going</u> to Judy's before we go to the party?
> <u>How about using</u> my car?

● 'Let's' followed by the base form of a verb

> <u>Let's go</u> outside.
> <u>Let's hope</u> we're lucky with the weather on holiday.

● 'Why don't I', 'Why don't you' or 'Why don't we' followed by the base form of a verb

> <u>Why don't I pick</u> you <u>up</u> at seven?
> <u>Why don't you write</u> to her yourself?
> <u>Why don't we just give</u> them what they have asked for?

Suggestions

- 'Why not' followed by the base form of a verb

  <u>*Why not bring*</u> *him along?*
  <u>*Why not try*</u> *both?*

Main points

You use 'Would you like' to offer something to someone or to invite them to do something.

You use 'Can I', 'Could I', and 'Shall I' when you offer to help someone.

1. When you are offering something to someone, or inviting them to do something, you use 'Would you like'.

> *Would you like* a drink?
> *Would you like* to come over to my house for a meal?
> *Would you like* me to take you home?

You can use 'Will you' to offer something to someone you know quite well, or to give an invitation in a fairly informal way.

> *Will you* have another biscuit, Dave?
> *Will you* come to my birthday party on Saturday night?

Offers and invitations

2 You use 'Can I' or 'Could I' when you are offering to do something for someone. 'Could I' is more polite.

> *Can I help you with the dishes?*
> *Could I help you carry those bags?*

You also use 'Shall I' when you are offering to do something, especially if you are fairly sure that your offer will be accepted.

> *Shall I shut the door?*
> *Shall I spell that for you?*

3 You use 'I can' or 'I could' to make an offer when you want to say that you are able to help someone.

> *I have a car. I can take Daisy and Peter to the station.*
> *I could pay some of the rent.*

4 You also use 'I'll' to offer to do something.

> *I'll give them a ring if you like.*
> *I'll show you the hotel.*

5 You use 'You must' if you want to invite someone very persuasively to do something.

> *You must come round for a meal some time next week.*
> *You must come and visit me.*

6 There are other ways of making offers and giving invitations without using modals. For example, you can use 'Let me' when offering to help someone.

> *Let me take you to your room.*
> *Let me drive you to London.*

You can make an offer or give an invitation in a more informal way by using an imperative sentence, when it is clear that you are not giving an order.

> *Have a cigar.*
> *Come to my place.*

You can add emphasis by putting 'do' in front of the verb.

> *Do have a chocolate biscuit.*
> *Do help yourselves.*
> *Do come in, Mr Travis.*

Offers and invitations

You can also give an invitation by using 'Why don't you' or 'How about'.

> *Why don't you* come to lunch tomorrow?
> *How about* coming with us to the party?
> *How about* you come and have dinner with me tonight?

Wants and wishes

Main points

You use 'would like' to say what you want.

You use 'wouldn't like' to say what you do not want.

You use 'would rather' or 'would sooner' to say what you prefer.

You also use 'wouldn't mind' to say what you want.

1 You can say what someone wants by using 'would like' followed by a 'to'-infinitive or a noun group.

>   I _would like_ to know the date of the next meeting.
>   John _would like_ his book back.

When the subject is a pronoun, you often use the short form '-'d' instead of 'would'.

>   I_'d like_ more information about the work you do.
>   We_'d like_ seats in the non-smoking section, please.

Wants and wishes

In spoken English, you can also use the short form '-'d' instead of 'would' when the subject is a noun.

> Sally'<u>d like</u> to go to the circus.

2 You can say what someone does not want by using 'would not like' or 'wouldn't like'.

> I <u>would not like</u> to see it.
> They <u>wouldn't like</u> that.

3 You use 'would like' followed by 'to have' and a past participle to say that someone wishes now that something had happened in the past, but that it did not happen.

> I <u>would like to have felt</u> more relaxed.
> She'<u>d like to have heard</u> me first.

You use 'would have liked', followed by a 'to'-infinitive or a noun group, to say that someone wanted something to happen, but it did not happen.

> Perhaps he <u>would have liked</u> to be a teacher.
> I <u>would have liked</u> more ice cream.

Note the difference. 'Would like to have' refers to present wishes about past events. 'Would have liked' refers to past wishes about past events.

Wants and wishes

4 You can also use 'would hate', 'would love', or 'would prefer', followed by a 'to'-infinitive or a noun group.

> I _would hate_ to have to move to another house now.
> I _would prefer_ a cup of coffee.

Note that 'would enjoy' is followed by a noun group or an '-ing' form, not by a 'to'-infinitive.

> I _would enjoy a bath_ before we go to the theatre.
> I _would enjoy seeing_ him again.
> I_'d enjoy_ working with him.

5 You can use 'would rather' or 'would sooner' followed by the base form of a verb to say that someone prefers one situation to another.

> I _would rather_ be happy than rich.
> He_'d rather_ be playing golf than sitting at his desk.
> I_'d sooner_ walk than take the bus.

Wants and wishes

6 You use 'I wouldn't mind', followed by an '-ing' form or a noun group, to say that you would like to do or have something.

> I *wouldn't mind* being the manager of a store.
> I *wouldn't mind* a cup of tea.

Main points

You use 'have to', 'must', and 'mustn't' to talk about obligation and necessity in the present and future.

You use 'had to' to talk about obligation and necessity in the past.

You use the auxiliary 'do' with 'have to' to make questions.

You use 'have got to' in informal English.

1 When you want to say that someone has an obligation to do something, or that it is necessary for them to do it, you use 'must' or 'have to'.

> *You <u>must</u> come to the meeting tomorrow.*
> *The plants <u>must</u> have plenty of sunshine.*
> *I enjoy parties, unless I <u>have to</u> make a speech.*
> *He <u>has to</u> travel to find work.*

2 There is sometimes a difference between 'must' and 'have to'. When you are stating your own opinion that something is an obligation or a necessity, you normally use 'must'.

> *I <u>must</u> be very careful not to upset him.*

Obligation and necessity 1

> *We <u>must</u> eat before we go.*
> *He <u>must</u> stop working so hard.*

When you are giving information about what someone else considers to be an obligation or a necessity, you normally use 'have to'.

> *They <u>have to</u> pay the bill by Thursday.*
> *She <u>has to</u> go now.*

Note that you normally use 'have to' for things that happen repeatedly, especially with adverbs of frequency such as 'often', 'always', and 'regularly'.

> *I always <u>have to</u> do the shopping.*
> *You often <u>have to</u> wait a long time for a bus.*

3 You use 'must not' or 'mustn't' to say that it is important that something is not done or does not happen.

> *You <u>must not</u> talk about politics.*
> *They <u>mustn't</u> find out that I came here.*

Note that 'must not' does not mean the same as 'not have to'. If you 'must not' do something, it is important that you do not do it.

If you 'do not have to' do something, it is not necessary for you to do it, but you can do it if you want.

⊖ WARNING: You only use 'must' for obligation and necessity in the present and the future.

Obligation and necessity 1

When you want to talk about obligation and necessity in the past, you use 'had to' rather than 'must'.

> *She <u>had to</u> catch the six o'clock train.*
> *I <u>had to</u> wear a suit.*

4 You use 'do', 'does', or 'did' when you want to make a question using 'have to' and 'not have to'.

> *How often <u>do</u> you <u>have to</u> buy petrol for the car?*
> *<u>Does</u> he <u>have to</u> take so long to get ready?*
> *What <u>did</u> you <u>have to</u> do?*
> *<u>Don't</u> you <u>have to</u> be there at one o'clock?*

⊖ WARNING: You do not normally form questions like these by putting a form of 'have' before the subject. For example, you do not normally say 'How often have you to buy petrol?'

5 In informal English, you can use 'have got to' instead of 'have to'.

> *You'<u>ve</u> just <u>got to</u> make sure you tell him.*
> *She'<u>s got to</u> see the doctor.*
> *<u>Have</u> you <u>got to</u> go so soon?*

⊖ WARNING: You normally use 'had to', not 'had got to', for the past.

> *He <u>had to</u> know.*
> *I <u>had to</u> lend him some money.*

6 You can only use 'have to', not 'must', if you are using another modal, or if you want to use an '-ing' form, a past participle, or a 'to'-infinitive.

> *They <u>may have to</u> be paid by cheque.*
> *She grumbled a lot about <u>having to</u> stay abroad.*
> *I would have <u>had to</u> go through London.*
> *He doesn't like <u>to have to</u> do the same job every day.*

Obligation and necessity 2

Main points

You use 'need to' to talk about necessity.

You use 'don't have to', 'don't need to', 'haven't got to', or 'needn't' to say that it is not necessary to do something.

You use 'needn't' to give someone permission not to do something.

You use 'need not have', 'needn't have', 'didn't need to', or 'didn't have to' to say that it was not necessary to do something in the past.

1 You can use 'need to' to talk about the necessity of doing something.

> You might <u>need to</u> see a doctor.
> A number of questions <u>need to</u> be asked.

2 You use 'don't have to' when there is no obligation or necessity to do something.

> Many women <u>don't have to</u> work.
> You <u>don't have to</u> learn any new typing skills for the job.

Obligation and necessity 2

You can also use 'don't need to', 'haven't got to', or 'needn't' to say that there is no obligation or necessity to do something.

> *You <u>don't need to</u> buy anything.*
> *I <u>haven't got to</u> go to work today.*
> *I can pick John up later on tonight. You <u>needn't</u> bother.*

3 You also use 'needn't' when you are giving someone permission not to do something.

> *You <u>needn't</u> say anything if you really don't want to.*
> *You <u>needn't</u> stay any longer tonight.*

4 You use 'need not have' or 'needn't have' and a past participle to say that someone did something which was not necessary. You are often implying that the person did not know at the time that their action was not necessary.

> *He <u>need not have</u> bothered to return early.*
> *The boys <u>needn't have</u> waited until the game began.*
> *Nell <u>needn't have</u> worked.*
> *We <u>needn't have</u> worried about our lack of experience.*

Unit 90

Obligation and necessity 2

5 You use 'didn't need to' to say that something was not necessary, and that it was known at the time that the action was not necessary. You do not know if the action was done, unless you are given more information.

> I *didn't need* to worry.
> They *didn't need* to talk about it, he already knew.

6 You also use 'didn't have to' to say that it was not necessary to do something.

> He *didn't have to* speak.
> As a matter of fact, Bill and I *didn't have to* pay.

7 You cannot use 'must' to refer to the past, so when you want to say that it was important that something did not happen or was not done, you use other expressions.

You can say 'It was important not to', or use phrases like 'had to make sure' or 'had to make certain' in a negative sentence.

It was <u>important</u> not to take the game too seriously.

It was <u>necessary</u> that no one was aware of being watched.

You <u>had to make sure</u> that you didn't spend too much.

We <u>had to</u> do our best to <u>make certain</u> that it wasn't out of date.

Mild obligation and advice

Main points

You use 'should' and 'ought' to talk about mild obligation.

You use 'should have' and 'ought to have' to say that there was a mild obligation to do something in the past, but it was not done.

You can also use 'had better' to talk about mild obligation.

1. You can use 'should' and 'ought' to talk about a mild obligation to do something. When you use 'should' and 'ought', you are saying that the feeling of obligation is not as strong as when you use 'must'.

'Should' and 'ought' are very common in spoken English.

'Should' is followed by the base form of a verb, but 'ought' is followed by a 'to'-infinitive.

When you want to say that there is a mild obligation not to do something, you use 'should not', 'shouldn't', 'ought not', or 'oughtn't'.

Mild obligation and advice

2 You use 'should' and 'ought' in three main ways:

● when you are talking about what is a good thing to do, or the right thing to do.

> *We __should__ send her a postcard.*
> *We __shouldn't__ spend all the money.*
> *He __ought__ to come more often.*
> *You __ought not__ to see him again.*

● when you are trying to advise someone about what to do or what not to do.

> *You __should__ claim your pension 3-4 months before you retire.*
> *You __shouldn't__ use a detergent.*
> *You __ought__ to get a new TV.*
> *You __oughtn't__ to marry him.*

● when you are giving or asking for an opinion about a situation. You often use 'I think', 'I don't think', or 'Do you think' to start the sentence.

> *I think that we __should__ be paid more.*
> *I don't think we __ought__ to grumble.*
> *Do you think he __ought not__ to go?*
> *What do you think we __should__ do?*

3 You use 'should have' or 'ought to have' and a past participle to say that there was a mild obligation to do something in the past, but that it was not

done. For example, if you say 'I should have given him the money yesterday', you mean that you had a mild obligation to give him the money yesterday, but you did not give it to him.

> I _should have_ finished my drink and gone home.
> You _should have_ realised that he was only joking.
> We _ought to have_ stayed in tonight.
> They _ought to have_ taken a taxi.

You use 'should not have' or 'ought not to have' and a past participle to say that it was important not to do something in the past, but that it was done. For example, if you say 'I should not have left the door open', you mean that it was important that you did not leave the door open, but you did leave it open.

> I _should not have_ said that.
> You _shouldn't have_ given him the money.
> They _ought not to have_ told him.
> She _oughtn't to have_ sold the ring.

4 You use 'had better' followed by a base form to indicate mild obligation to do something in a particular situation. You also use 'had better' when giving advice or when giving your opinion about something. The negative is 'had better not'.

Mild obligation and advice

I think I <u>had better</u> show this to you now.
You'<u>d better</u> go tomorrow.
I'<u>d better not</u> look at this.

⊖ WARNING: The correct form is always 'had better' (not 'have better'). You do not use 'had better' to talk about mild obligation in the past, even though it looks like a past form.

Main points

You use defining relative clauses to say exactly which person or thing you are talking about.

Defining relative clauses are usually introduced by a relative pronoun such as 'that', 'which', 'who', 'whom', or 'whose'.

A defining relative clause comes immediately after noun, and needs a main clause to make a complete sentence.

[1] You use defining relative clauses to give information that helps to identify the person or thing you are talking about.

> The man <u>who you met yesterday</u> was my brother.
> The car <u>which crashed into me</u> belonged to Paul.

When you are talking about people, you use 'that' or 'who' in the relative clause.

> He was the man <u>that</u> bought my house.
> You are the only person here <u>who</u> knows me.

Defining relative clauses

When you are talking about things, you use 'that' or 'which' in the relative clause.

> *There was ice cream <u>that</u> Mum had made herself.*
> *I'll tell you the first thing <u>which</u> I can remember.*

2 | 'That', 'who', or 'which' can be:

● the subject of the verb in the relative clause

> *The thing <u>that</u> surprised me was his attitude.*
> *The woman <u>who</u> lives next door is very friendly.*
> *The car <u>which</u> caused the accident drove off.*

● the object of the verb in the relative clause

> *The thing <u>that</u> I really liked about it was its size.*
> *The woman <u>who</u> you met yesterday lives next door.*
> *The car <u>which</u> I wanted to buy was not for sale.*

In formal English, 'whom' is used instead of 'who' as the object of the verb in the relative clause.

> *She was a woman <u>whom</u> I greatly respected.*

3 | You can leave out 'that', 'who', or 'which' when they are the object of the verb in the relative clause.

> *The woman you met yesterday lives next door.*
> *The car I wanted to buy was not for sale.*
> *The thing I really liked about it was its size.*

Defining relative clauses

🚫 WARNING: You cannot leave out 'that', 'who', or 'which' when they are the subject of the verb in the relative clause. For example, you say 'The woman who lives next door is very friendly'. You do not say 'The woman lives next door is very friendly'.

4 A relative pronoun in a relative clause can be the object of a preposition. Usually the preposition goes at the end of the clause.

> *I wanted to do the job <u>which</u> I'd been training <u>for.</u>*
> *The house <u>that</u> we lived <u>in</u> was huge.*

You can often omit a relative pronoun that is the object of a preposition.

> *Angela was the only person <u>I could talk to.</u>*
> *She's the girl <u>I sang the song for.</u>*

The preposition always goes in front of 'whom', and in front of 'which' in formal English.

> *These are the people <u>to whom</u> Catherine was referring.*
> *He was asking questions <u>to which</u> there were no answers.*

5 You use 'whose' in relative clauses to indicate who something belongs to or relates to. You normally

Defining relative clauses

use 'whose' for people, not for things.

> *A child <u>whose</u> mother had left him was crying loudly.*
> *We have only told the people <u>whose</u> work is relevant to this project.*

6 You can use 'when', 'where', and 'why' in defining relative clauses after certain nouns. You use 'when' after 'time' or time words such as 'day' or 'year'. You use 'where' after 'place' or place words such as 'room' or 'street'. You use 'why' after 'reason'.

> *There had been <u>a time when</u> she hated all men.*
> *This is <u>the year when</u> profits should increase.*
> *He showed me <u>the place where</u> they work.*
> *That was <u>the room where</u> I did my homework.*
> *There are several <u>reasons why</u> we can't do that.*

Main points

You use non-defining relative clauses to give extra information about the person or thing you are talking about.

Non-defining relative clauses must be introduced by a relative pronoun such as 'which', 'who', 'whom', or 'whose'.

A non-defining relative clause comes immediately after a noun and needs a main clause to make a complete sentence.

1 You use non-defining relative clauses to give extra information about the person or thing you are talking about. The information is not needed to identify that person or thing.

> *Professor Marvin, <u>who was always early,</u> was there already.*

'Who was always early' gives extra information about Professor Marvin. This is a non-defining relative clause, because it is not needed to identify the person you are talking about. We already know that you are talking about Professor Marvin.

Note that in written English, a non-defining rela-

Non-defining clauses

tive clause is usually separated from the main clause by a comma, or by two commas.

> *I went to the cinema with Mary, who you met.*
> *British Rail, which has launched an enquiry, said one coach was badly damaged.*

2 You always start a non-defining relative clause with a relative pronoun. When you are talking about people, you use 'who'. 'Who' can be the subject or object of a non-defining relative clause.

> *Heath Robinson, <u>who</u> died in 1944, was a graphic artist and cartoonist.*
> *I was in the same group as Janice, <u>who</u> I like a lot.*

In formal English, 'whom' is sometimes used instead of 'who' as the object of a non-defining relative clause.

> *She was engaged to a sailor, <u>whom</u> she had met at Dartmouth.*

3 When you are talking about things, you use 'which' as the subject or object of a non-defining relative clause.

> *I am teaching at the Selly Oak centre, <u>which</u> is just over the road.*
> *He was a man of considerable inherited wealth, <u>which</u> he ultimately spent on his experiments.*

⊖ WARNING: You do not normally use 'that' in non-defining relative clauses.

4 You can also use a non-defining relative clause beginning with 'which' to say something about the whole situation described in a main clause.

> *I never met Brando again, <u>which</u> was a pity.*
> *She was a little tense, <u>which</u> was understand-able.*
> *Small computers need only small amounts of power, <u>which</u> means that they will run on small batteries.*

5 When you are talking about a group of people or things and then want to say something about only some of them, you can use one of the following expressions:

many of which	many of whom
none of which	none of whom
one of which	one of whom
some of which	some of whom

> *They were all friends, <u>many of whom</u> had known each other for years.*
> *He talked about several very interesting people, <u>some of whom</u> he was still in contact with.*

Non-defining clauses

6 | You can use 'when' and 'where' in non-defining relative clauses after expressions of time or place.

> *This happened in 1957, <u>when</u> I was still a baby.*
> *She has just come back from a holiday in Crete,*
> *<u>where</u> Alex and I went last year.*

Participle clauses

Main points

Nouns are followed by '-ing' clauses that say what a person or thing is doing.

Nouns are followed by '-ed' clauses that show that a person or thing has been affected or caused by an action.

1. You can often give more information about a noun, or an indefinite pronoun such as 'someone' or 'something', by adding a clause beginning with an '-ing' form, an '-ed' form, or a 'to'-infinitive.

> *He gestured towards <u>the box lying on the table</u>.*
> *I think <u>the idea suggested by Tim</u> is the best one.*
> *She wanted <u>someone to talk to</u>.*

2. You use an '-ing' clause after a noun to say what someone or something is doing or was doing at a particular time.

> *The young girl <u>sitting opposite him</u> was his daughter.*
> *Most of the people <u>strolling in the park</u> were teenagers.*

Participle clauses

3 You can also use an '-ing' clause after a noun to say what a person or thing does generally, rather than at a particular time.

> *Problems <u>facing parents</u> should be discussed.*
> *The men <u>working there</u> were not very friendly.*

4 You often use an '-ing' clause after a noun which is the object of a verb of perception, such as 'see', 'hear', or 'feel'.
> See also Unit 72.

> *Suddenly we saw Amy <u>walking down the path.</u>*
> *He heard a distant voice <u>shouting.</u>*
> *I could feel something <u>touching my face and neck,</u> something ice-cold.*

5 You use an '-ed' clause after a noun to show that someone or something has been affected or caused by an action.

> *He was the new minister <u>appointed by the President.</u>*
> *The man <u>injured in the accident</u> was taken to hospital.*

Remember that not all verbs have regular '-ed' forms.

> *A story <u>written by a young girl</u> won the competition.*
> *She was wearing a dress <u>bought in Paris.</u>*

Main points

Some adjectives can be used after nouns.

You can use relative clauses after nouns.

Adverbials of place and time can come after nouns.

A noun can be followed by another noun group.

You can use 'that'-clauses after some nouns.

1. You can use some adjectives after a noun to give more information about it, but the adjectives are usually followed by a prepositional phrase, a 'to'-infinitive clause, or an adverbial.

> *This is a warning to people <u>eager for a quick profit.</u>*
> *These are the weapons <u>likely to be used.</u>*
> *For a list of the facilities <u>available here,</u> ask the secretary.*
> *You must talk to the people <u>concerned.</u>*

➤ See Unit 31 for more information on adjectives used after nouns.

Adding to a noun group

2 When you want to give more precise information about the person or thing you are talking about, you can use a defining relative clause after the noun.

> *The man <u>who had done it</u> was arrested.*
> *There are a lot of things <u>that are wrong.</u>*
> *Nearly all the people <u>I used to know</u> have gone.*

Note that you can also use defining relative clauses after indefinite pronouns such as 'someone' or 'something'.

> *I'm talking about somebody <u>who is really ill.</u>*

➤ See Unit 92 for more information on defining relative clauses.

3 You can use an adverbial of place or time after a noun.

> *People <u>everywhere</u> are becoming more selfish.*
> *This is a reflection of life <u>today.</u>*

4 You can add a second noun group after a noun. The second noun group gives you more precise information about the first noun.

> *Her mother, <u>a Canadian,</u> died when she was six.*

Note that the second noun group is separated by commas from the rest of the clause.

Unit 95

5 Nouns such as 'advice', 'hope', and 'wish', which refer to what someone says or thinks, can be followed by a 'that'-clause. Here are some examples:

advice	agreement	belief	claim
conclusion	decision	feeling	hope
promise	threat	warning	wish

> *It is my firm <u>belief that</u> more women should stand for Parliament.*
>
> *I had a <u>feeling that</u> no-one thought I was good enough.*

Note that all these nouns are related to reporting verbs, which also take a 'that'-clause. For example, 'information' is related to 'inform', and 'decision' is related to 'decide'.

Some of these nouns can also be followed by a 'to'-infinitive clause.

agreement	decision	hope	order
promise	threat	warning	wish

> *The <u>decision to go</u> had not been an easy one.*
>
> *I reminded Barnaby of his <u>promise to buy his son a horse.</u>*

Adding to a noun group

6 A few other nouns can be followed by a 'that'-clause.

advantage	confidence	danger	effect
evidence	fact	idea	impression
news	opinion	possibility	view

> He didn't want her to get the <u>idea that</u> he was rich.
>
> I had no <u>evidence that</u> Jed was the killer.
>
> He couldn't believe the <u>news that</u> his house had just burned down.

Note that when a noun group is the object of a verb, it may be followed by different structures.

➤ See Units 69 to 72 for more information.

Time clauses

Main points

You use time clauses to say when something happens.

Time clauses can refer to the past, present, or future.

Time clauses are introduced by words such as 'after', 'when', or 'while'.

A time clause needs a main clause to make a complete sentence. The time clause can come before or after the main clause.

1 You use time clauses to say when something happens. The verb in the time clause can be in a present or a past tense.

> *I look after the children <u>while</u> she <u>goes</u> to London.*
> *I haven't given him a thing to eat <u>since</u> he <u>arrived.</u>*

⊖ WARNING: You never use a future tense in a time clause. You use one of the present tenses instead.

Time clauses

> *Let me stay here <u>till</u> Jeannie <u>comes</u> to bed.*
> *I'll do it <u>when</u> I'<u>ve finished</u> writing this letter.*

2 When you want to say that two events happen at the same time, you use a time clause with 'as', 'when', or 'while'.

> *We arrived <u>as they were leaving.</u>*

Sometimes the two events happen together for a period of time.

> *She wept bitterly <u>as she told her story.</u>*

Sometimes one event interrupts another event.

> *He was having his dinner <u>when</u> the telephone rang.*
> *John will arrive <u>while</u> we are watching the film.*

Note that you often use a continuous tense for the interrupted action.
➤ See Unit 60.

3 When you want to say that one event happens before or after another event, you use a time clause with 'after', 'as soon as', 'before', or 'when'.

> *<u>As soon as</u> we get tickets, we'll send them to you.*
> *Can I see you <u>before</u> you go, Helen?*
> *<u>When</u> he had finished reading, he looked up.*

Time clauses

Note that you use the past perfect to indicate an event that happened before another event in the past.

4 When you want to mention a situation which started in the past and continued until a later time, you use a time clause with 'since' or 'ever since'. You use a past simple or a past perfect in the time clause, and a past perfect in the main clause.

> He hadn't cried <u>since he was</u> a boy of ten.
> Janine had been busy <u>ever since she had heard</u> the news.
> I'<u>d wanted</u> to come ever since I was a child.

If the situation started in the past and still continues now, you use a past simple in the time clause, and a present perfect in the main clause.

> I've been in politics <u>since I was</u> at university.
> Ever since you arrived <u>you've been causing</u> trouble.

Note that after impersonal 'it' and a time expression, if the main clause is in the present tense, you use 'since' with a past simple.

> It <u>is</u> two weeks now since I <u>wrote</u> to you.

If the main clause is in the past tense, you use 'since' with a past perfect.

Time clauses

It was nearly seven years since I'd seen Toby.

➤ For 'since' as a preposition, see Unit 40.

5 When you want to talk about when a situation ends, you use a time clause with 'till' or 'until' and a present or past tense.

> *We'll support them till they find work.*
> *I stayed there talking to them until I saw Sam.*
> *She waited until he had gone.*

6 When you want to say that something happens before or at a particular time, you use a time clause with 'by the time' or 'by which time'.

> *By the time I went to bed, I was exhausted.*
> *He came back later, by which time they had gone.*

7 In written or formal English, if the subject of the main clause and the time clause are the same, you sometimes omit the subject in the time clause and use a participle as the verb.

> *I read the book before going to see the film.*
> *The car was stolen while parked in a London street.*

Purpose and reason clauses

Main points

Purpose clauses are introduced by conjunctions such as 'so', 'so as to', 'so that', 'in order to' or 'in order that'.

Reason clauses are introduced by conjunctions such as 'as', 'because', or 'in case'.

A purpose or reason clause needs a main clause to make a complete sentence.

A purpose clause usually comes after a main clause. A reason clause can come before or after a main clause.

1 You use a purpose clause when you are saying what someone's intention is when they do something. The most common type of purpose clause is a 'to'-infinitive clause.

> *The children sleep together <u>to keep</u> warm.*
> *They locked the door <u>to stop</u> us from getting in.*

Instead of using an ordinary 'to'-infinitive, you often use 'in order to' or 'so as to' with an infinitive.

> *He gave up his job <u>in order to stay</u> at home.*
> *I keep the window open, <u>so as to let</u> fresh air in.*

392

Purpose and reason clauses

To make a purpose clause negative, you have to use 'in order not to' or 'so as not to' with an infinitive.

> *I would have to give myself something to do <u>in order not to</u> be bored.*
> *They went on foot, <u>so as not to</u> be heard.*

Another way of making purpose clauses negative is by using 'to avoid' with an '-ing' form or a noun group.

> *I had to turn away <u>to avoid letting</u> him see my smile.*
> *They drove through town <u>to avoid the motor-way.</u>*

2 Another type of purpose clause begins with 'in order that', 'so', or 'so that'. These clauses usually contain a modal.

When the main clause refers to the present, you usually use 'can', 'may', 'will', or 'shall' in the purpose clause.

> *Any holes should be fenced <u>so that</u> people <u>can't</u> fall down them.*
> *I have drawn a diagram <u>so that</u> my explanation <u>will</u> be clearer.*

When the main clause refers to the past, you usually use 'could', 'might', 'should', or 'would' in the purpose clause.

Purpose and reason clauses

> She said she wanted tea ready at six <u>so</u> she
> <u>could</u> be out by eight.
> Someone lifted Philip onto his shoulder <u>so that</u>
> he <u>might</u> see the procession.

You use 'in order that', 'so', and 'so that', when the
subject of the purpose clause is different from the
subject of the main clause. For example, you say
'I've underlined it so that it will be easier.' You do
not say 'I've underlined it to be easier'.

3 You can also talk about the purpose of an action
by using a prepositional phrase introduced by
'for'.

> She went out <u>for a run.</u>
> They said they did it <u>for fun.</u>
> I usually check, just <u>for safety's sake.</u>

4 You use a reason clause when you want to explain
why someone does something or why it happens.
When you are simply giving the reason for something, you use 'because', 'since', or 'as'.

> I couldn't see Helen's expression, <u>because</u> her
> head was turned.
> <u>Since</u> it was Saturday, he stayed in bed.
> <u>As</u> he had been up since 4 am, he was very tired.

Purpose and reason clauses

You can also use 'why' and a reported question to talk about the reason for an action.

➤ See Unit 75.

> *I asked him <u>why</u> he had come.*

5 When you are talking about a possible situation which explains the reason why someone does something, you use 'in case' or 'just in case'.

> *I've got the key <u>in case</u> we want to go inside.*
> *I am here <u>just in case</u> anything unusual happens.*

⊖ WARNING: You do not use a future tense after 'in case'. You do not say 'I'll stay behind in case she'll arrive later'.

Main points

You use result clauses to talk about the result of an action or situation.

Result clauses are introduced by conjunctions such as 'so', 'so…(that)', or 'such…(that)'.

A result clause needs a main clause to make a complete sentence. The result clause always comes after the main clause.

1. You use 'so' and 'so that' to say what the result of an action or situation is.

> *He speaks very little English, <u>so</u> I talked to him through an interpreter.*
> *My suitcase had become damaged on the journey home, <u>so that</u> the lid would not stay closed.*

2. You also use 'so…that' or 'such…that' to talk about the result of an action or situation.

> *He dressed <u>so</u> quickly <u>that</u> he put his boots on the wrong feet.*
> *She got <u>such</u> a shock <u>that</u> she dropped the bag.*

'That' is often omitted.

Result clauses

> *They were <u>so</u> surprised they didn't try to stop him.*
>
> *They got <u>such</u> a fright they ran away again.*

3 You only use 'such' before a noun, with or without an adjective.

> *They obeyed him with <u>such willingness</u> that the strike went on for over a year.*
>
> *Sometimes they say <u>such stupid things</u> that I don't even bother to listen.*

If the noun is a singular count noun, you put 'a' or 'an' in front of it.

> *I was in <u>such a panic</u> that I didn't know it was him.*

Note that you only use 'so' before an adjective or an adverb.

> *It all sounded <u>so crazy</u> that I laughed out loud.*
>
> *They worked <u>so quickly</u> that there was no time for talking.*

4 When you want to say that a situation does not happen because someone or something has an excessive amount of a quality, you use 'too' with an adjective and a 'to'-infinitive. For example, if you say 'They were too tired to walk', you mean that they did not walk because they were too tired.

Result clauses

He was <u>too proud to apologise.</u>
She was <u>too weak to lift</u> me.

You also use 'too' with an adverb and a 'to'-infinitive.

They had been walking <u>too silently to be heard.</u>
She spoke <u>too quickly</u> for me <u>to understand.</u>

5 When you want to say that a situation happens or is possible because someone or something has a sufficient amount of a quality, you use 'enough' after adjectives and adverbs, followed by a 'to'-infinitive.

He was <u>old enough to understand.</u>
I could see <u>well enough to know</u> we were losing.

You normally put 'enough' in front of a noun, not after it.

I don't think I've got <u>enough information to speak</u> confidently.

6 You also use 'and as a result', 'and so', or 'and therefore' to talk about the result of an action or situation.

He had been ill for six months, <u>and as a result</u> had lost his job.
She was having difficulty getting her car out, <u>and so</u> I had to move my car to let her out.

Result clauses

We have a growing population <u>and therefore</u> we need more and more food.

You can also put 'therefore' after the subject of the clause. For example, you can say 'We have a growing population and we therefore need more food'.

'As a result' and 'therefore' can also be used at the beginning of a separate sentence.

In a group, they are not so frightened. <u>As a result,</u> patients reveal their problems more easily.
He lacks money to invest in improving his tools. <u>Therefore</u> he is poor.

Main points

These are clauses introduced by 'although', 'in spite of' and 'though'.

You use contrast clauses when you want to make two statements, and one statement makes the other seem surprising.

Contrast clauses are introduced by conjunctions such as 'although', 'in spite of', or 'though'.

A contrast clause needs a main clause to make a complete sentence. The contrast clause can come before or after the main clause.

1 When you simply want to contrast two statements, you use 'although', 'though' or 'even though'.

> *Although* he was late, he stopped to buy a sandwich.
> *Though* he has lived for years in London, he writes in German.
> I used to love listening to her, *even though* I could only understand about half of what she said.

Contrast clauses

Sometimes you use words like 'still', 'nevertheless', or 'just the same' in the main clause to add emphasis to the contrast.

> *Although* I was shocked, I <u>still</u> couldn't blame him.
> *Although* his company is profitable, it <u>nevertheless</u> needs to face up to some serious problems.
> *Although* she hated them, she agreed to help them <u>just the same.</u>

When the subject of the contrast clause and the main clause are the same, you can often omit the subject and the verb 'be' in the contrast clause.

> *Although poor,* we still have our pride.
> (Although we are poor…)
> *Though dying of cancer,* he painted every day.
> (Though he was dying of cancer…)

2 Another way of making a contrast is to use 'despite' or 'in spite of', followed by a noun group.

> *Despite the difference* in their ages they were close friends.
> *In spite of poor health,* my father was always cheerful.

Contrast clauses

⊖ WARNING: You say 'in spite of' but 'despite' without 'of'.

> *His mind was still extremely active, <u>in spite of</u> his age.*
> *Henry enjoys exceptionally good health, <u>despite</u> his age.*

3 You can also use an '-ing' form after 'despite' or 'in spite of'.

> *<u>Despite working</u> hard, I failed all my university exams.*
> *Conservative MPs are against tax rises, <u>in spite of wanting</u> lower inflation.*

4 You can also use 'despite the fact that' or 'in spite of the fact that', followed by a clause.

> *<u>Despite the fact that</u> it sounds like science fiction, most of it is technically possible at this moment.*
> *They ignored this order, <u>in spite of the fact that</u> they would probably get into a great deal of trouble.*

Contrast clauses

It is possible to omit 'that', especially in spoken English.

He insisted on playing, <u>in spite of the fact he had a bad cold.</u>

<u>Despite the fact they live in the same city,</u> they lead very different lives.

Manner clauses

Main points

You use manner clauses to talk about how something is done.

Manner clauses are introduced by conjunctions such as 'as', 'as if', 'as though', or 'like'.

A manner clause needs a main clause to make a complete sentence. The manner clause always comes after the main clause.

1 When you want to say how someone does something, or how something is done, you use 'as'.

> He behaves <u>as</u> he does, because his father was really cruel to him.
> The bricks are made <u>as</u> they were in Roman times.

You often use 'just', 'exactly', or 'precisely' in front of 'as' for emphasis.

> It swims on the sea floor <u>just as</u> its ancestors did.
> I like to plan my day <u>exactly as</u> I want.
> Everything went <u>precisely as</u> she had planned.

2 When you want to indicate that the information in the manner clause might not be true, or is definitely not true, you use 'as if' or 'as though'.

Manner clauses

> *Almost <u>as if</u> she'd read his thought, she straight-ened her back and returned to her seat.*
> *Just act <u>as though</u> everything's normal.*

After 'as if' or 'as though', you often use a past tense even when you are talking about the present, to emphasize that the infomation in the manner clause is not true. In formal English, you use 'were' instead of 'was'. ➤ See also Unit 68.

3 You also use 'the way (that)', 'in a way (that)', or 'in the way (that)' to talk about how someone does something, or how something is done.

> *I was never allowed to sing <u>the way</u> I wanted to.*
> *They did it <u>in a way that</u> I hadn't seen before.*
> *We make it move <u>in the way that</u> we want it to.*

4 You can use 'how' in questions and reported questions to talk about the method used to do something, and sometimes to indicate your surprise that it was possible to do it.

> *'<u>How</u> did he get in?' – 'He broke a window.'*
> *I wondered <u>how</u> he could afford a new car.*

Sometimes, you can use 'how' to talk about the manner in which someone does something.

> *I watched <u>how</u> he did it, then tried to copy him.*
> *Tell me <u>how</u> he reacted when he saw you.*

Main points

You can sometimes change the focus of a sentence by moving part of the sentence to the front.

You can also change the focus of a sentence by using an expression such as 'The fact is', 'The thing is', or 'The problem is'.

You can also use impersonal 'it' to change the focus of a sentence.

1. In most affirmative clauses, the subject of the verb comes first.

> *They* went to Australia in 1956.
> *I've* no idea who it was.

However, when you want to emphasize another part of the sentence, you can put that part first instead.

> *In 1956* they went to Australia.
> *Who it was* I've no idea.

2. One common way of giving emphasis is by placing an adverbial at the beginning of the sentence.

Changing sentence focus

> *At eight o'clock* I went downstairs for my
> breakfast.
> *For years* I'd had to hide what I was thinking.

Note that after adverbials of place and negative
adverbials, you normally put the subject after the
verb.

> *She rang the bell for Sylvia. In came a girl she
> had not seen before.*
> *On no account must they be let in.*

After adverbials of place, you can also put the subject before the verb. You must do so, if the subject
is a pronoun.

> *The door opened and in she came.*
> *He'd chosen Japan, so off we went to the
> Japanese Embassy.*

3 When you want to say that you do not know something, you can put a reported question at the
beginning of the sentence.

> *What I'm going to do next I don't quite know.*
> *How he managed I can't imagine.*

4 Another way of focusing on information is to use a
structure which introduces what you want to say
by using 'the' and a noun, followed by 'is'.

The nouns most commonly used in this way are:

answer	conclusion	fact	point
problem	question	rule	solution
thing	trouble	truth	

The second part of the sentence is usually a 'that'-clause or a 'wh'-clause, although it can also be a 'to'-infinitive clause or a noun group.

> *The problem is* that she can't cook.
> *The thing is,* how are we going to get her out?
> *The solution is* to adopt the policy which will produce the greatest benefits.
> *The answer is* planning, timing, and, above all, practical experience.

It is also common to use a whole sentence to introduce information in following sentences.

➜ See Unit 102 for more information.

5 You can also focus on information by using impersonal 'it', followed by 'be', a noun group, and a relative clause.

The noun group can be the subject or object of the relative clause.

> *It was Ted who* broke the news to me.
> *It is* usually *the other vehicle that* suffers most.

Changing sentence focus

> *It's money that they want.*
> *It was me Dookie wanted.*

There are many other ways of focusing on information:

> *Ted was the one who broke the news to me.*
> *Money is what we want.*
> *What we want is money.*

6 You can also focus on the information given in the other parts of a clause, or a whole clause, using impersonal 'it'. In this case, the second part of the sentence is a 'that'-clause.

> *It was from Francis that she first heard the news.*
> *It was meeting Peter that really started me off on this new line of work.*
> *Perhaps it's because he's a misfit that I get along with him.*

Main points

You can use pronouns and determiners to refer back to something that has already been mentioned.

You use coordinating conjunctions to link clauses.

1 When you speak or write, you usually need to make some connection with other things that you are saying or writing. The most common way of doing this is by referring back to something that has already been mentioned.

2 One way of referring back to something is to use a personal pronoun such as 'she', 'it', or 'them', or a possessive pronoun such as 'mine' or 'hers'.

> *My father* is fat. *He* weighs over fifteen stone.
> *Mary* came in. *She* was a good-looking woman.
> 'Have you been to *London* ?' – 'Yes, *it* was very crowded.'
> 'Have you heard of *David Lodge* ?' – 'Yes, I've just read a novel of *his.*'
> 'Would you mind moving *your car*, please?' – 'It's not *mine.*'

Cohesion

3 You can also use a specific determiner such as 'the' or 'his' in front of a noun to refer back to something.

> *A <u>man</u> and a <u>woman</u> were walking up the hill. <u>The</u> man wore shorts, a T-shirt, and basketball sneakers. <u>The</u> woman wore a print dress.*
> *'Thanks,' said Brody. He put the telephone down, turned out the light in <u>his</u> office, and walked out to <u>his</u> car.*

4 The demonstratives 'this', 'that', 'these' and 'those' are also used to refer back to a thing or fact that has just been mentioned.

> *In 1973 he went on a <u>caravan holiday</u>. At the beginning of <u>this</u> holiday he began to experience pain in his chest.*
> *There's a lot of <u>material</u> there. You can use some of <u>that.</u>*

5 The following general determiners can also be used to refer back to something:

> another both each either every neither other

> *Five <u>officials</u> were sacked. <u>Another</u> four were arrested.*
> *There are more than two hundred and fifty <u>species of shark,</u> and <u>every</u> one is different.*

Cohesion

6 Another common way of making connections in spoken or written English is by using one of the following coordinating conjunctions:

and	but	nor	or	so	then	yet

Anna had to go into town <u>and</u> she wanted to go to Bride Street.

I asked if I could borrow her bicycle <u>but</u> she refused.

He was only a boy then, <u>yet</u> he was not afraid.

You can use a coordinating conjunction to link clauses that have the same subject. When you link clauses which have the same subject, you do not always need to repeat the subject in the second clause.

She was born in Budapest <u>and</u> raised in Manhattan.

He didn't yell <u>or</u> scream.

When she saw Morris she went pale, <u>then</u> blushed.

7 Most subordinating conjunctions can also be used to link sentences together, rather than to link a subordinate clause with a main clause in the same sentence.

'When will you do it?' – '<u>When</u> I get time.'

Cohesion

'Can I borrow your car?' – *'<u>So long as</u> you drive carefully.'*

We send that by airmail. <u>Therefore</u>, it's away on Thursday and our client gets it on Monday.

8 When people are speaking or writing, they often use words that refer back to similar words, or words that refer back to a whole sentence or paragraph.

Everything was <u>quiet</u>. Everywhere there was the <u>silence</u> of the winter night.

<u>'What are you going to do?'</u> – 'That's a good <u>question.'</u>

GLOSSARY OF GRAMMAR TERMS

abstract noun a noun used to refer to a quality, idea, feeling, or experience, rather than a physical object; **eg** *size, reason, joy*.
➤ See Units 15, 70, 73

active voice verb groups such as 'gives', 'took', 'has made', which are used when the subject of the verb is the person or thing doing the action or responsible for it. Compare with **passive voice**.
➤ See Unit 78

adjective a word used to tell you more about a person or thing, such as their appearance, colour, size, or other qualities; **eg** ... *a **pretty blue** dress*.
➤ See Units 31–36, 47

adjunct another name for **adverbial**.

adverb a word that gives more information about when, how, where, or in what circumstances something happens; **eg** *quickly, now*.
➤ See Units 21, 36–44, 95

adverbial an adverb, or an adverb phrase, prepositional phrase, or noun group which does the same job as an adverb; **eg** *then, very quickly, in the street, the next day*.
➤ See Units 38–46

Glossary

adverbial of degree an adverbial which indicates the amount or extent of a feeling or quality; eg *She felt **extremely** tired*.
➤ See Unit 43

adverbial of duration an adverbial which indicates how long something continues or lasts; eg *He lived in London **for six years***.
➤ See Unit 42

adverbial of frequency an adverbial which indicates how often something happens; eg *She **sometimes** goes to the cinema*.
➤ See Unit 41

adverbial of manner an adverbial which indicates the way in which something happens or is done; eg *She watched **carefully***.
➤ See Unit 39

adverbial of place an adverbial which gives more information about position or direction; eg *They are **upstairs**… Move **closer***.
➤ See Unit 44–45

adverbial of probability an adverbial which gives more information about how sure you are about something; eg *I realized I'd **probably** lost it*.
➤ See Unit 41

adverbial of time an adverbial which gives more

Glossary

information about when something happens;
eg *I saw her **yesterday***.
➤ See Unit 40

adverb phrase two adverbs used together; eg *She spoke **very quietly**… He did not play **well enough** to win.*
➤ See Unit 38

affirmative a clause or sentence in the affirmative is one which does not contain a negative word such as 'not' and which is not a question.
➤ See Units 21, 29–30, 41–42

apostrophe s an ending ('s) added to a noun to indicate possession; eg *…Harriet**'s** daughter… the professor**'s** husband… the Managing Director**'s** secretary.*
➤ See Units 21–22

article See **definite article, indefinite article**.

auxiliary another name for **auxiliary verb**.

auxiliary verb one of the verbs 'be', 'have', and 'do' when they are used with a main verb to form tenses, negatives, and questions. Some grammars include modals in the group of auxiliary verbs.
➤ See Units 3, 5, 7, 9–11, **57**

base form the form of a verb without any endings

added to it, which is used in the 'to'–infinitive and for the imperative; **eg** *walk, go, have, be*.
The base form is the form you look up in a dictionary.
➤ See Units 3, 72, 79

cardinal number a number used in counting; **eg** *one, seven, nineteen*.
➤ See Units 2, 13, 23, 26, 30–31

clause a group of words containing a verb. See also **main clause** and **subordinate clause**.
➤ See Unit 1

collective noun a noun that refers to a group of people or things, which can be used with a singular or plural verb; **eg** *committee, team, family*.
➤ See Unit 14

comparative an adjective or adverb with '–er' on the end or 'more' in front of it; **eg** *slower, more important, more carefully*.
➤ See Units 35–36

complement a noun group or adjective, which comes after a link verb such as 'be', and gives more information about the subject of the clause; **eg** *She is a **teacher**… She is **tired***.
➤ See Units 1–3, 73

complex sentence a sentence consisting of a main clause and a subordinate clause; **eg** *She wasn't*

Glossary

thinking very quickly because she was tired.
➤ See Unit 1

compound sentence a sentence consisting of two or more main clauses linked by 'and', 'or' or 'but'; eg *They picked her up and took her straight into the house.*
➤ See Unit 1

conditional clause a subordinate clause, usually starting with 'if' or 'unless', which is used to talk about possible situations and their results; eg *They would be rich **if they had taken my advice**... We'll go to the park, **unless it rains**.*
➤ See Units 66–67

conjunction a word such as 'and', 'because', or 'nor', that links two clauses, groups, or words.
➤ See Units 1, 97, 102

continuous tense a tense which contains a form of the verb 'be' and a present participle; eg *She **was laughing**... They **had been playing** badminton.* See **tense**.
➤ See Unit 60

contrast clause a subordinate clause, usually introduced by 'although' or 'in spite of the fact that', which contrasts with a main clause; eg ***Although I like her,** I find her hard to talk to.*
➤ See Unit 99

Glossary

coordinating conjunction a conjunction such as 'and', 'but', or 'or', which links two main clauses.
➤ See Unit 102

countable noun another name for **count noun**.

count noun a noun which has both singular and plural forms; eg *dog/dogs, foot/feet lemon/lemons*.
➤ See Units 13, 24, 26–27, 29–30

declarative another name for **affirmative**.

defining relative clause a relative clause which identifies the person or thing that is being talked about; eg *…the lady **who lives next door**… I wrote down everything **that she said**.* Compare with **non-defining relative clause**.
➤ See Unit 92

definite article the determiner 'the'.
➤ See Units 24–25

delexical verb a common verb such as 'give', 'have', 'make', or 'take', which has very little meaning in itself and is used with a noun as object that describes the action; eg *She **gave** a small cry… I've just **had** a bath.*
➤ See Unit 56

demonstrative one of the words 'this', 'that', these', and 'those'; eg *…**this** woman. …**that** tree… **That** looks interesting… **This** is fun.*
➤ See Unit 19

Glossary

descriptive adjective an adjective which describes a person or thing, for example indicating their size, age, shape, or colour, rather than expressing your opinion of that person or thing. Compare with **opinion adjective**.
➤ See Unit 32

determiner one of a group of words including 'the', 'a', 'some', and 'my', which are used at the beginning of a noun group.
➤ See Units 2, 13–14, 23–30

direct object a noun group referring to the person or thing affected by an action, in a clause with a verb in the active voice; eg *She wrote **her name**... I shut **the windows***.
➤ See Units 16, 20, 51–53

direct speech the actual words spoken by someone.
➤ See Units 74–77

ditransitive verb another name for a verb with two objects, such as 'give', 'take', or 'sell'; eg *She **gave** me a kiss*.
➤ See Unit 52

double-transitive verb another name for a **ditransitive verb**.

'-ed' adjective an adjective which has the same form as the '–ed' form of a regular verb, or the past

participle of an irregular verb; eg …***boiled*** potatoes.
…*a **broken** wing*.
→ See Unit 34

'-ed' form the form of a regular verb used for the
past simple and for the past participle.
→ See Units 3, 57, 94

ellipsis the leaving out of words when they are
obvious from the context.

emphasizing adverb an adverb such as
'absolutely' or 'utterly', which modifies adjectives
that express extreme qualities, such as 'astonishing'
and 'wonderful'; eg *You were **absolutely**
wonderful*.
→ See Unit 43

ergative verb a verb which is both transitive and
intransitive in the same meaning. The object of the
transitive use is the subject of the intransitive use;
eg *He **boiled** a kettle… The kettle **boiled***.
→ See Unit 55

first person see **person**.

future tense see **tense**.

gerund another name for the '–ing' form when it is
used as a noun.
→ See Units 69, 71–72

Glossary

'if'-clause see **conditional clause**.

imperative the form of a verb used when giving orders and commands, which is the same as its base form; eg *Come* here… *Take* two tablets every four hours… *Enjoy* yourself.
 ➤ See Units **4**, 8, 12, 66

impersonal 'it' 'it' used as an impersonal subject to introduce new information; eg *It's raining… **It's** ten o'clock.*
 ➤ See Units 16–17, 33, 47, 73, 76, 96, 101

indefinite adverb a small group of adverbs including 'anywhere' and 'somewhere' which are used to indicate place in a general way.
 ➤ See Unit 21

indefinite article the determiners 'a' and 'an'.
 ➤ See Unit 26

indefinite pronoun a small group of pronouns including 'someone' and 'anything' which are used to refer to people or things without saying exactly who or what they are.
 ➤ See Units **21**, 94–95

indirect object an object used with verbs that take two objects. For example, in 'I gave him the pen' and 'I gave the pen to him', 'him' is the indirect

Glossary

object and 'pen' is the direct object. Compare with **direct object**.
➤ See Units 16, 20, 52

indirect question a question used to ask for information or help; eg *Do you know **where Jane is?**… I wonder **which hotel it was**.*
➤ See Unit 9

indirect speech the words you use to report what someone has said, rather than using their actual words. Also called **reported speech**.
➤ See Units 74–77

infinitive the base form of a verb; eg *I wanted to **go**… She helped me **dig** the garden.* The infinitive is the form you look up in a dictionary.
➤ See Units 11, 33–34, 65, 70, 73, 76–77, 79, 82, 91, 95, 97–98

'-ing' adjective an adjective which has the same form as the present participle of a verb; eg …*a **smiling** face.* …*a **winning** streak.*
➤ See Unit 34

'-ing' form a verb form ending in '–ing' which is used to form verb tenses, and as an adjective or a noun. Also called the **present participle**.
➤ See Units 3, 34, 69, 71–72, 94

interrogative pronoun one of the pronouns

Glossary

'who', 'whose', 'whom', 'what', and 'which', when they are used to ask questions.
➤ See Unit 6

interrogative sentence a sentence in the form of a question.
➤ See Unit 5

intransitive verb a verb which does not take an object; eg *She **arrived**… I **was yawning***. Compare with **transitive verb**.
➤ See Unit 51

irregular verb a verb that has three or five forms, or whose forms do not follow the normal rules.
➤ See Unit 3 and appendix of verb tables

link verb a verb which takes a complement rather than an object; eg *be, become, seem, appear*.
➤ See Unit 73

main clause a clause which does not depend on another clause, and is not part of another clause.
➤ See Unit 1

main verb all verbs which are not auxiliaries or modals.
➤ See Units 3, 5, 57

manner clause a subordinate clause which describes the way in which something is done,

usually introduced with 'as' or 'like'; eg *She talks **like her mother used to***.
➔ See Units 68, 100

modal a verb such as 'can', 'might', or 'will', which is always the first word in a verb group and is followed by the base form of a verb. Modals are used to express requests, offers, suggestions, wishes, intentions, politeness, possibility, probability, certainty, obligation, and so on.
➔ See Units 7–8, 18, 60–61, 64, 67, **79-91**, 97

mood the mood of a clause is the way in which the verb forms are used to show whether the clause is a statement, command, or question.

negative a negative clause, question, sentence, or statement is one which has a negative word such as 'not', and indicates the absence or opposite of something, or is used to say that something is not the case; eg *I don't know you… I'll never forget.*
Compare with **positive**.
➔ See Units 4, **11-12**, 57, 80

negative word a word such as 'never', 'no', 'not', 'nothing', or 'nowhere', which makes a clause, question, sentence, or statement negative.
➔ See Units 3–4, 7–8, 10–**12**, 21, 23, 27, 30, 80

non-defining relative clause a relative clause which gives more information about someone or

Glossary

something, but which is not needed to identify them because we already know who or what they are; eg *That's Mary,* **who was at university with me.** Compare with **defining relative clause**.
➤ See Unit 93

non-finite clause a 'to'–infinitive clause, '–ed' clause, or '–ing' clause.
➤ See Units 69–73, 94

noun a word which refers to people, things, ideas, feelings, or qualities; eg *woman, Harry, guilt.*
➤ See Units 2, **13-15**, 23–31, 48, 56, 94–95

noun group a group of words which acts as the subject, complement, or object of a verb, or as the object of a preposition.
➤ See Units 1–**2**, 38–40, 44

object a noun group which refers to a person or thing that is affected by the action described by a verb or preposition. Compare with **subject**.
➤ See Units 16, 20, **51-56**

object pronoun one of a set of pronouns including 'me', 'him', and 'them', which are used as the object of a verb or preposition. Object pronouns are also used as complements after 'be'; eg *I hit* **him**... *It's* **me**.
➤ See Unit 16

opinion adjective an adjective which you use to

express your opinion of a person or thing, rather
than just describing them. Compare with
descriptive adjective.
➤ See Unit 32

ordinal number a number used to indicate where
something comes in an order or sequence;
eg *first, fifth, tenth, hundredth.*

participle a verb form used for making different
tenses. Verbs have two participles, a present
participle and a past participle.
➤ See Units 3, 34, 57, 69, 71–72, 94

particle an adverb or preposition which combines
with verbs to form phrasal verbs.
➤ See Unit 50

passive voice verb groups such as 'was given',
'were taken', 'had been made', which are used
when the subject of the verb is the person or thing
that is affected by the action. Compare with **active
voice**.
➤ See Units 70, **78**

past form the form of a verb, often ending in '–ed',
which is used for the past simple tense.
➤ See Units 3, 59

past participle a verb form which is used to form
perfect tenses and passives. Some past participles

are also used as adjectives; **eg** *watched, broken.*
➤ See Units 3, 57, 70, 94

past tense see **tense.**

perfect tense see **tense**.

person one of the three classes of people who can be involved in something that is said. The person or people who are speaking or writing are called the first person ('I', 'we'). The person or people who are listening or reading are called the second person ('you'). The person, people or things that are being talked about are called the third person('he', 'she', 'it', 'they').

personal pronoun one of the group of words including 'I', 'you', and 'me', which are used to refer back to yourself, the people you are talking to, or the people or things you are talking about. See also **object pronoun** and **subject pronoun**.
➤ See Units **16**, 102

phrasal verb a combination of a verb and a particle, which together have a different meaning to the verb on its own; **eg** *back down, hand over, look forward to.*
➤ See Units **50**, 69

plural the form of a count noun or verb, which is used to refer to or talk about more than one person

Glossary

or thing; eg *Dogs have ears*… *The women were outside.*
➤ See Units 2, 13–14

plural noun a noun which is normally used only in the plural form; eg *trousers, scissors.*
➤ See Unit 14

positive a positive clause, question, sentence, or statement is one which does not contain a negative word such as 'not'. Compare with **negative.**
➤ See Units 21, 29–30, 41–42

possessive one of the determiners 'my', 'your', 'his', 'her', 'its', 'our', or 'their', which is used to show that one person or thing belongs to another; eg …*your car.*
➤ See Units **22**–23

possessive adjective another name for **possessive**.
➤ See Units **22**–23

possessive pronoun one of the pronouns 'mine', 'yours', 'hers', 'his', 'ours', or 'theirs'.
➤ See Units **22**, 37

preposition a word such as 'by', 'with' or 'from', which is always followed by a noun group.
➤ See Units 5, 16, 20, **44-50**, 52, 54, 92

Glossary

prepositional phrase a structure consisting of a preposition followed by a noun group as its object; eg *on the table, by the sea.*
➤ See Units 22, 34, 36, 38–40, 43, 46–49, 97

present participle see **'-ing' form**.

present tense see **tense**.

progressive tense another name for **continuous tense**.
➤ See Unit 60

pronoun a word which you use instead of a noun, when you do not need or want to name someone or something directly; eg *it, you, none.*
➤ See Units 6, **16–17**, 19–22, 37, 92–95, 102

proper noun a noun which is the name of a particular person, place, organization, or building. Proper nouns are always written with a capital letter; eg *Nigel, Edinburgh, the United Nations, Christmas.*
➤ See Unit 25

purpose clause a subordinate clause which is used to talk about the intention that someone has when they do something; eg *I came here **in order to ask you out to dinner.***
➤ See Unit 97

qualifier a word or group of words, such as an

Glossary

adjective, prepositional phrase, or relative clause,
which comes after a noun and gives more
information about it; eg ...*the person **involved**.
...a book **with a blue cover**. ...the shop **that I went
into**.*
➤ See Units 22, 92–94

question a sentence which normally has the verb in
front of the subject, and which is used to ask
someone about something; eg *Have you any
money?*
➤ See Units **5–10**, 11, 58, 75, 80

question tag an auxiliary or modal with a pronoun,
which is used to turn a statement into a question.
eg *He's very friendly, **isn't he**?... I can come, **can't I?***
➤ See Units 7–8

reason clause a subordinate clause, usually
introduced by 'because', 'since', or 'as', which is used to
explain why something happens or is done;
eg ***Since you're here,** we'll start.*
➤ See Unit 97

reciprocal verb a verb which describes an action
which involves two people doing the same thing to
each other; eg *I **met** you at the dance... We've **met**
one another before... They **met** in the street.*
➤ See Unit 54

reflexive pronoun a pronoun ending in '–self' or

Glossary

'–selves', such as 'myself' or 'themselves', which you use as the object of a verb when you want to say that the object is the same person or thing as the subject of the verb in the same clause; **eg** *He hurt **himself**.*
➤ See Unit 20

reflexive verb a verb which is normally used with a reflexive pronoun as object; **eg** *He **contented himself** with the thought that he had the only set of keys to the car.*
➤ See Unit 53

regular verb a verb that has four forms, and follows the normal rules.
➤ See Unit 3

relative clause a subordinate clause which gives more information about someone or something mentioned in the main clause. See also **defining relative clause** and **non-defining relative clause**.
➤ See Units **92-93**, 95

relative pronoun 'that' or a 'wh'–word such as 'who' or 'which', when it is used to introduce a relative clause; **eg** *…the girl **who** was carrying the bag.*
➤ See Units 92–93

reported clause the clause in a report structure

which indicates what someone has said; eg *She said that I couldn't see her.*
➤ See Units 74–77

reported question a question which is reported using a report structure rather than the exact words used by the speaker. See also **indirect question**.
➤ See Unit 75

reported speech the words you use to report what someone has said, rather than using their actual words. Also called **indirect speech**.
➤ See Units 74–77

reporting clause the clause in a report structure which contains the reporting verb.
➤ See Units 74, 76

reporting verb a verb which describes what people say or think; eg *suggest, say, wonder.*
➤ See Units 74, 76–77

report structure a structure which is used to report what someone says or thinks, rather than repeating their exact words; eg *She told me she'd be late.*
➤ See Units 74–77

result clause a subordinate clause introduced by 'so', 'so…that', or 'such…(that)', which indicates the result of an action or situation; eg *I don't think there's*

Glossary

*any more news, **so I'll finish.***
➤ See Unit 98

second person see **person**.

semi-modal a term used by some grammars to refer to the verbs 'dare', 'need', and 'used to', which behave like modals in some structures.
➤ See Units 63, 72, 90

sentence a group of words which express a statement, question, or command. A sentence usually has a verb and a subject, and may be a simple sentence with one clause, or a compound or complex sentence with two or more clauses. In writing, a sentence has a capital letter at the beginning and a full-stop, question mark, or exclamation mark at the end.
➤ See Units 1, 66, 92–93, 96–102

short form a form in which one or more letters are omitted and two words are joined together, for example an auxiliary or modal and 'not', or a subject pronoun and an auxiliary or modal; **eg** *aren't, couldn't, he'd, I'm, it's, she's.*
➤ See Unit 11

simple tense a present or past tense formed without using an auxiliary verb; **eg** *...I **wait**. ...she **sang**.* See **tense**.
➤ See Units 58–63, 65

Glossary

singular the form of a count noun or verb which is used to refer to or talk about one person or thing; eg *A **dog was** in the **car**… That **woman is** my **mother***.
➤ See Units 13–14

singular noun a noun which is normally used only in the singular form; eg *the sun, a bath*.
➤ See Unit 14

strong verb another name for **irregular verb**.

subject the noun group in a clause that refers to the person or thing who does the action expressed by the verb; eg ***We** were going shopping*. Compare with **object**.
➤ See Units 1, 3, 5, 9–10, 13, 15–18, 21, 25, 38, 53, 55, 69–71, 75–77, 80, 102

subject pronoun one of the set of pronouns including 'I', 'she', and 'they', which are used as the subject of a verb.
➤ See Unit 16

subordinate clause a clause which must be used with a main clause and is not usually used alone, for example a time clause, conditional clause, relative clause, or result clause, and which begins with a subordinating conjunction such as 'because' or 'while'.
➤ See Units 1, 66–68, 92–93, 96–100, 102

subordinating conjunction a conjunction such

Glossary

as 'although', 'as if', 'because' or 'while', which you use to begin a subordinate clause; **eg** *He laughed as if he'd said something funny.*
➤ See Unit 102

superlative an adjective or adverb with '–est' on the end or 'most' in front of it; **eg** *thinnest, quickest, most beautiful.*
➤ See Units 32, **35-36**, 70

tag question a statement to which a question tag has been added; **eg** *She's quiet, isn't she?… You've got a car, haven't you?*
➤ See Units 7–8

tense the form of a verb which shows whether you are referring to the past, present, or future.
➤ See Units 57–65

future 'will' or 'shall' with the base form of the verb, used to refer to future events; **eg** *She **will come** tomorrow… **I shall** ask her as soon as I see her.*
➤ See Unit 64

future continuous 'will' or 'shall' with 'be' and a present participle, used to refer to future events; **eg** *She **will be going** soon.*
➤ See Units 60, 64

future perfect 'will' or 'shall' with 'have' and a past participle, used to refer to future events; **eg** *I **shall***

Glossary

have finished by tomorrow.
➤ See Units 61, 64

future perfect continuous 'will' or 'shall' with 'have been' and a present participle, used to refer to future events; eg I **will have been walking** for three hours by then.
➤ See Units 60–61, 64

past simple the past form of a verb, used to refer to past events; eg They **waited**.
➤ See Units 59, 63, 74

past continuous 'was' or 'were' with a present participle, usually used to refer to past events; eg They **were worrying** about it all day yesterday.
➤ See Units 59–60, 63

past perfect 'had' with a past participle, used to refer to past events; eg She **had finished** her meal.
➤ See Units 59, 61, 63

past perfect continuous 'had been' with a present participle, used to refer to past events; eg He **had been waiting** for hours.
➤ See Units 59–61, 63

present simple the base form and the third person singular form of a verb, usually used to refer to present events; eg I **like** bananas… My sister **hates** them.
➤ See Units 58, 62, 65, 74

Glossary

present continuous the present simple of 'be' with a present participle, usually used to refer to present events; eg *Things **are improving**… She **is working***.
➤ See Units 58, 60, 62, 65

present perfect 'have' or 'has' with a past participle, used to refer to past events which exist in the present; eg *She **has loved** him for over ten years*.
➤ See Units 58, 61, 63, 65

present perfect continuous 'have been' or 'has been' with a present participle, used to refer to past events which continue in the present; eg *We **have been sitting** here for hours*.
➤ See Units 58, 60–61, 63

'that'-clause a clause starting with 'that', used mainly when reporting what someone has said; eg *She said **that she'd wash up for me***.
➤ See Units 33–34, 76–77, 95

third person see **person**.

time clause a subordinate clause which indicates the time of an event; eg *I'll phone you **when I get back***.
➤ See Unit 96

time expression a noun group used as an

adverbial of time; **eg** *last night, the day after tomorrow, the next time.*
➤ See Unit 40

'to'-infinitive the base form of a verb preceded by 'to'; **eg** *to go, to have, to jump.*
➤ See Units 11, 33–34, 65, 70–73, 76–77, 79, 82, 91, 95, 97–98

transitive verb a verb which takes an object; **eg** *She's **wasting** her money.* Compare with **intransitive verb**.
➤ See Unit 51

uncountable noun another name for **uncount noun**.

uncount noun a noun which has only one form, takes a singular verb, and is not used with 'a' or numbers. Uncount nouns often refer to substances, qualities, feelings, activities, and abstract ideas; **eg** *coal, courage, anger, help, fun.*
➤ See Units **15**, 24, 27, 29–30

verb a word which is used with a subject to say what someone or something does, or what happens to them; **eg** *sing, spill, die.*
➤ See Units 3–4, 10, 49–65, 69–78

verb group a main verb, or a main verb with one or more auxiliaries, a modal, or a modal and an

Glossary

auxiliary, which is used with a subject to say what someone does, or what happens to them; eg I**'ll show** them… She**'s been** sick.
➤ See Units 1, **3**, 5, 11–12, 57, 79

'wh'-question a question which expects the answer to give more information than just 'yes' or 'no'; eg *What happened next?… Where did he go?* Compare with **'yes/no'-question**.
➤ See Units 5–**6**, 9, 75

'wh'-word one of a group of words starting with 'wh–', such as 'what', 'when' or 'who', which are used in 'wh'–questions. 'How' is also called a 'wh'–word because it behaves like the other 'wh'–words.
➤ See Units 5–**6**, 70, 75, 77, 92–93

'yes/no'-question a question which can be answered by just 'yes' or 'no', without giving any more information; eg *Would you like some more tea?* Compare with **'wh'-question**.
➤ See Units 5, 7, 10, 75

IRREGULAR VERBS

INFINITIVE	PAST TENSE	PAST PARTICIPLE
arise	arose	arisen
awake	awoke	awoken
be	was, were	been
bear	bore	born(e)
beat	beat	beaten
begin	began	begun
bend	bent	bent
bet	bet, betted	bet, betted
bind	bound	bound
bite	bit	bitten
bleed	bled	bled
blow	blew	blown
break	broke	broken
breed	bred	bred
bring	brought	brought
build	built	built
burn	burnt, burned	burnt, burned
burst	burst	burst
buy	bought	bought
can	could	(been able)
cast	cast	cast
catch	caught	caught
choose	chose	chosen
cling	clung	clung
come	came	come
cost	cost	cost
creep	crept	crept
cut	cut	cut
deal	dealt	dealt

Irregular verbs

INFINITIVE	PAST TENSE	PAST PARTICIPLE
dig	dug	dug
do (does)	did	done
draw	drew	drawn
dream	dreamed, dreamt	dreamed, dreamt
drink	drank	drunk
drive	drove	driven
eat	ate	eaten
fall	fell	fallen
feed	fed	fed
feel	felt	felt
fight	fought	fought
find	found	found
fling	flung	flung
fly	flew	flown
forbid	forbad(e)	forbidden
forecast	forecast	forecast
forget	forgot	forgotten
forgive	forgave	forgiven
freeze	froze	frozen
get	got	got, *(US)* gotten
give	gave	given
go (goes)	went	gone
grind	ground	ground
grow	grew	grown
hang	hung	hung
hang *(execute)*	hanged	hanged
have	had	had
hear	heard	heard
hide	hid	hidden
hit	hit	hit
hold	held	held
hurt	hurt	hurt

Irregular verbs

INFINITIVE	PAST TENSE	PAST PARTICIPLE
keep	kept	kept
kneel	knelt, kneeled	knelt, kneeled
know	knew	known
lay	laid	laid
lead	led	led
lean	leant, leaned	leant, leaned
leap	leapt, leaped	leapt, leaped
learn	learnt, learned	learnt, learned
leave	left	left
lend	lent	lent
let	let	let
lie (lying)	lay	lain
light	lit, lighted	lit, lighted
lose	lost	lost
make	made	made
may	might	–
mean	meant	meant
meet	met	met
mistake	mistook	mistaken
mow	mowed	mown, mowed
must	(had to)	(had to)
pay	paid	paid
put	put	put
quit	quit, quitted	quit, quitted
read	read	read
rid	rid	rid
ride	rode	ridden

Irregular verbs

INFINITIVE	PAST TENSE	PAST PARTICIPLE
ring	rang	rung
rise	rose	risen
run	ran	run
saw	sawed	sawed, sawn
say	said	said
see	saw	seen
sell	sold	sold
send	sent	sent
set	set	set
sew	sewed	sewn
shake	shook	shaken
shear	sheared	shorn, sheared
shed	shed	shed
shine	shone	shone
shoot	shot	shot
show	showed	shown
shrink	shrank	shrunk
shut	shut	shut
sing	sang	sung
sink	sank	sunk
sit	sat	sat
sleep	slept	slept
slide	slid	slid
sling	slung	slung
slit	slit	slit
smell	smelt, smelled	smelt, smelled
sow	sowed	sown, sowed
speak	spoke	spoken
speed	sped, speeded	sped, speeded

Irregular verbs

INFINITIVE	PAST TENSE	PAST PARTICIPLE
spell	spelt, spelled	spelt, spelled
spend	spent	spent
spill	spilt, spilled	spilt, spilled
spin	spun	spun
spit	spat	spat
spoil	spoiled, spoilt	spoiled, spoilt
spread	spread	spread
spring	sprang	sprung
stand	stood	stood
steal	stole	stolen
stick	stuck	stuck
sting	stung	stung
stink	stank	stunk
stride	strode	stridden
strike	struck	struck
swear	swore	sworn
sweep	swept	swept
swell	swelled	swollen, swelled
swim	swam	swum
swing	swung	swung
take	took	taken
teach	taught	taught
tear	tore	torn
tell	told	told
think	thought	thought
throw	threw	thrown
thrust	thrust	thrust
tread	trod	trodden
wake	woke, waked	woken, waked